THE PRESSURE
TRAP

Other Books by Heather Lindsey

Pink Lips & Empty Hearts
A Perfect Recipe
The Runaway Bride
Dusty Crowns: Dusting Yourself Off and Breaking
Free from the Distractions to be Who God Called
You to be
The Purpose Room
Fighting Together
Silent Seasons

Available now on Amazon, Audible and
https://www.pinkypromiseboutiques.com/books/

THE PRESSURE

TRAP

BREAKING FREE FROM THE PRESSURES OF SOCIETY TO BECOME WHO GOD CALLED YOU TO BE

HEATHER LINDSEY

DEDICATION

To my mama, Linda Canter & my mother-in-love, Clover Lindsey. Two of the most encouraging women that never pressured me to be anything other than what God called me to be.

CONTENTS

FOREWORD

It is hard to escape the pressures that surround each of us on a daily basis. Some of these forces are glaring, but others are more subtle, they are a constant demeaning and detracting undercurrent. I don't always like who I am under pressure, yet at the same time I've learned to be thankful for the revelation.

In so many ways I've learned to view the exposing effect of pressure as a gift.

We can't avoid the pressures of life, but we can choose how we will respond to them.

Will we cave in and allow the outward and inward pressures to freeze us and halt our forward progress? Will we turn back to the trappings of our past patterns and ways of dealing with stress...alcohol, relationships or escapism? Or will we stand on God's word and allow the pressure to be a place of transformation?

> Fear not, for I have redeemed you; I have called you by name, you are mine. When you pass through the waters, I will be with you; and through the rivers, they shall not overwhelm you; when you walk through fire you shall not be burned, and the flame shall not consume you. Isaiah 43:1-2

We are guaranteed pressure. The same God who redeems us refines us. Outward pressure can yield inward transformation if we turn to Our Father in seasons of stress. I am so thankful that Heather has chosen to tackle this tough subject. I love her. I am honored to be in relationship with her. She writes from a place of authenticity and authority. I know, The Pressure Trap will be yet another tool in God's transformative process in your life.

Lisa Bevere

New York Times Best Selling Author

INTRODUCTION

Have you ever just been sick and tired of the pressure? The pressure to always have a plan. The pressure to have it all together. The pressure to look perfect, the pressure to get married, to have kids and to get the perfect job. The pressure to reach some unattainable image of who you are is exhausting!

I believe the enemy is the originator of this kind of pressure. The origin of all sin can be attributed to Satan pressuring Eve to eat the fruit in the Garden of Eden. For years and years, Satan has been subconsciously reminding us of trying to remind of us of what we don't have and what we are not doing. Then after the seed of pressure is planted by the enemy, it is fed by our own self-doubt, pressures from society, pressure from friends, family and even people we don't know, all in the hope of living up to some unrealistic expectation of ourselves.

What is pressure defined? Merriam-Webster defines it as:

- the burden of physical or mental distress
- the constraint of circumstance: the weight of social or economic imposition

Pressure is a burden. It's a burden that weighs us down physically, emotionally, mentally, and spiritually. After reading the definition of pressure, Psalm 55:22 immediately came to mind.

> Give your burdens to the Lord, and he will take care of you. He will not permit the godly to slip and fall.

I love that Jesus knew that we would get attacked with the burdens of this life and He already had a solution set up. He tells us, "*Give* your burdens to Me, I will take care of you."

Can I keep it real with you? I feel pressured to write at least one book a year.

I almost finished a book on marriage when the Lord told me to stop writing it for now. I recall sitting in my hotel room, frustrated.

"Lord, you haven't given me a title. I am feeling pressured and stressed out because I need to wrap up this book."

He said to me, "Who put that pressure on you?"

I was caught off guard with that question from the Lord. I knew He wasn't putting that pressure on me. But, it was coming from somewhere. I thought long and hard and said, "well, I guess me? The feeling that I need to constantly keep evolving forward. I mean, You always give me a book each year, Lord! I just feel pressured."

The Lord said to me, "That is exactly what I want you to write about: "The Pressure Trap." You're not the only person who is feeling the pressure to always have a new book, to get married, to have kids, to climb the corporate ladder, get to the right college and to have it all together.

I sat there, totally shocked. It made so much sense because I had not only made bad decisions in the past due to "pressure" but I almost put out this book on marriage due to "pressure."

I'm sure that I could have wrapped up that book on marriage in the flesh but I just didn't feel like it was *flowing.* I know this because I didn't feel the presence of the Holy Spirit over my words for this season. I'm sure I could have released that book and it would have been fine but I didn't want to force something that I *knew* God wasn't behind just to say I did it. With every book I've written, the Holy Spirit has led the way and I refuse to let the fabricated pressure I put on myself take me out of God's timing.

Have you ever done that? Fabricated and forced something because you didn't feel like you were enough? Got a boyfriend for the sake of getting one? Spent money you didn't have to impress a bunch of people that you don't really care for? Applied to go back to school because you felt purposeless? Lied to cover yourself from the opinions of people?

I could have easily finished that book and kept it moving. The book was 75% finished and it just made sense. *But, it didn't make faith.* I knew that God didn't tell me to release that book right now. It wasn't the season for it. But it is the season to remind people to stop allowing false pressures to distract them from where the Lord is leading them.

The days of you being led by your feelings are OVER. The days of you creating your own path just to say that you've accomplished something are OVER. The days of you comparing yourself against someone else are OVER. The days of you not feeling like you're enough are OVER. The days of you wishing that you were someone else, doing something else are OVER. The days of you allowing your family to control and dictate your life are OVER. The days of you being ashamed and guilty from your past are OVER.

I truly believe that the Holy Spirit will show you where you are pressuring yourself, the pressure you allow others to put on you AND the pressure you place on others. By the time you finish this book, I am confident that you will be so sure of God's timing and His ways that you won't acknowledge the pressures that this world tries to place on you. You will walk boldly in YOUR lane and do exactly what God is telling you to do.

CHAPTER ONE
FEELING PRESSURED?

It seems like everyone's favorite question to children is, "What do you want to be when you grow up?"

When I was in grade school, I felt the pressure to know the answer to this question. I had teachers, aunts, uncles and everyone else asking me, "What do you want to be when you grow up?" When I asked my four-year-old son, Logan, this question, he responded with the only answer that makes sense at his age, "I don't know, I am only four."

This poses the question of why we make a habit of putting so much pressure on children and teenagers to know their life's plan? Very few of us knew what we were going to grow up to be. I wanted to be an Olympic track star, then a veterinarian, then a police officer, then a lawyer, a psychologist and then a TV host.

So, yeah. I knew *exactly* what I wanted to be when I grew up. Ok, not really. A preacher, author and business owner was never in the picture.

The pressure to define ourselves in earthly ways starts before we even know our identity. It plants seeds in our heart that we need to have a "plan" but you're still growing, developing and trying to figure out who you are as a person.

By the time you get to high school you've sat through countless career days where you've been "exposed" to your options. And I'm sure this was right around the time your parents began asking, "Have you thought about college?"

They may ask, "What do you want to study?" but they're really asking, "How will you identify yourself in society?"

As teenagers we begin to LABEL and IDENTIFY ourselves based on what we DO and not who we are as people. If anything, we should have been asked, "What is your character like? Who are you as a person? Are you a liar? A thief? Are you lazy? Do you love Jesus? Are you sensitive to His spirit? Do you even care about other people? Are you selfish??"

These are the things we need to look at and cultivate versus, "What label do you want to have to cover up who you REALLY are as a person."

Who cares if you're a lawyer if you have bad character and you rip people off? Who cares if you're a doctor if you're mean and you look at child porn at night? Who cares if you think you're called to sing but you're inconsistent, you don't treat anyone right and you're selfish. I challenge you to look at your children and ask, "Who are you?" Not, "What do you want to be."

Maybe some of you have identified yourself based on a label that was given to you. "You're going to take over the family business" or, "You're going to be a doctor, just like your father." Maybe you felt the pressure of no one believing in you or the weight of your family's failures.

After you get harassed in high school about your career, you apply to college and you have to put your "projected major for school." I should have put "I don't know. I just got to the earth 17 years ago. I can't think clearly. I don't know what I want. I am terrible at choosing boyfriends, friends and just about everything else. I study to pass."

As we lay the foundation of being free from pressure, it's important that we recognize that God has specifically called each of us to do something on this earth. Once you know that you have a purpose then you won't give into the bait of being pressured to be anything other than what God has called you to be.

Jeremiah 1:5 tells us that while we were in our mother's womb, God designed us with purpose. You are not here by accident. There is something that you are specifically supposed to do here. Because we know that God has established a purpose for our lives, no person on this earth can change it to fit some social "norm."

Nonetheless, when you graduate college, the pressure is on to find a job. Maybe some of your friends found work right away from the internships they had while in college. You're expected to have it all together. Then, the student loan police come after you in about 6 months because they assume by then, you will have a job and everything figured out.

Six months after graduation I was getting evicted from my first apartment in New York. Talk about pressure! I'm supposed to be in the big city, "living it up" and working a great job but I wasn't. I had this image in my head of success. I had this plan of how I thought things would go and I pressured myself to obtain it. When my plan didn't work out, my identity was lost. This is why the pressure trap is dangerous

– it will have you measuring success on the basis of what you think instead of what God thinks. Everyone told me that having a degree meant that I would get a great job right out of school and that everything was going to be perfect. I would live in a fabulous loft and take a car service home every night. I had to quickly let that go because New York City didn't hand me anything. I had to work my face off.

I am not surprised that people reach a certain age and close down their practice, leave teaching, or go back to school to start a whole new career in their 40's. So many of us are miserable in the lives *we* chose because we made decisions based on society and pressures from family and friends.

I have a friend who is a doctor. While she was in medical school, I asked her if this was what God called her to do and if she would do it again if she had the chance. She told me that she didn't know what God called her to do but if she could turn back time, she would not become a doctor. Now she was "in too deep" between $300,000 in student loans and her degree – she felt she had no choice but to remain a doctor. My heart broke for her. She grew up very poor without a lot of support from family. The pressure to create a different life pushed her into a career that made a lot of money but did not fulfill her. So now, she will go to a job that she is not passionate about for the rest of her life because the pressure from the student loans and the pressure to never go back to that the life she lived as a child.

Now, this book is not about your purpose (see my book, The Purpose Room for that ☺) But let's just be clear, when you are doing what God has called you to do, you will experience more passion and joy than anything else in this world. You don't pursue a career for a paycheck. You pursue Jesus and He provides all of your needs according to His riches and glory.

I can assure you of this truth, throughout this season of my life falling apart in New York City, God developed my identity. When your plans and hopes crash around you and then you have people trying to pressure you and pull you in several directions, you quickly realize that your hope cannot be in this world. Trying to please everyone and be the perfect woman with the perfect story is exhausting. Truly surrendering this area of pressure to the Lord freed me to do what He has called me to do.

Even right now, I am preparing to give birth in a couple of months, I have my annual Pinky Promise Conference in Atlanta, GA in which I will be hosting it at 9 months pregnant. I am wrapping up this book, I will be recording an audio book, I need to get our new son's bedroom unpacked and organized and so much more. This is not including our several businesses, raising children, our church in Atlanta and so much more. I have so much on my plate that if I think about it, I get overwhelmed by the pressure to be perfect in every area.

Instead, I have truly let go of my life. We must all come to this realization in our walk with Jesus. It's where they recognize that the "work that is started in the Spirit cannot be finished in the flesh. (Galatians 3:3) So, instead of stressing out about my travel schedule and everything else – I simply have decided to take life one day at a time. Tomorrow has enough struggles, why pressure ourselves and allow others to pressure us when we could trust God with what he has given us? I believe that God graces us for today, not tomorrow. Then, when tomorrow comes, it will be today. I know who I am. I know whose I am. I know my identity. I don't rush ahead of God. I am thankful for His timing. I grew weary in trying to please everyone. And I pray that you are tired too. Tired enough to be free to be who God called you to be in your current season.

Once you conquer the foundation of worldly pressure, you know that we have already overcome by the BLOOD of the Lamb and the word of our testimony. Now, you cannot pressure me. Someone can try, but I will lovingly correct them. I know who

I am. I know whose I am. I know my identity. I don't rush ahead of God. I am thankful for His timing. I grew weary in trying to please everyone. I grew weary in trying to be the perfect wife, the perfect mother, the perfect businesswoman.

You cannot pressure me out of the will of God for my life and you cannot pressure me into another "will." I pray that as you read these chapters that the scales from the pressure of this world fall off of you and the Lord would give you a boldness to be free from this world's pressure.

CHAPTER TWO

WHO ARE YOU UNDER PRESSURE?

We must recognize that the external pressure we experience not only serves as a distraction but will undoubtedly reveal the position of our hearts. Who are you under pressure? What habits do you fall back to? What things do you say or affirm about yourself? Do you turn away from Jesus? What or who are you running to in the midst of pressure that puts a Band-Aid on your situation but doesn't completely heal the problem?

It seemed like every time the Lord tried to show Himself to me in the midst of a test, I would go and get another boyfriend. I would pick up another job or apply for grad school. Pressure made me run to external things for comfort. I didn't know this then but if I turned to God during those pressure filled times, when everything was ripped from under me, I would have been in the best possible place. The safest place. The arms of my Father.

I was just like the children of Israel. The second you left me alone, I was creating a golden statue to bow down and worship, questioning why God would lead me to a wilderness.

> Numbers 14:1-4 says, "That night all the members of the community raised their voices and wept aloud. All the Israelites grumbled against Moses and Aaron, and the whole assembly said to them, "If only we had died in Egypt! Or in this wilderness! Why is the Lord bringing us to this land only to let us fall by the sword? Our wives and children will be taken as plunder. Wouldn't it be better for us to go back to Egypt?" And they said to each other, "We should choose a leader and go back to Egypt."

Ever been in those shoes? Where it seems like you

are getting slammed left and right by tests and trials? Moses and Aaron were trying to encourage the Israelites to conquer a land but they were afraid. I was afraid of being single. I was afraid of not having money and being evicted again. I was afraid of not being successful so I ran back to grad school. When the pressure is put on, where do you run? Who do you run to? For the Israelites, they wanted to run back to Egypt but even in Egypt they were in great bondage. I was not comfortable when I was in disobedience and the enemy likes to create this fantasy that life was so amazing and much better "way back then." It proves to be a lie every time.

Let me just tell on myself. I met a guy who was an NBA player during those first months of me moving to New York. I made it clear that I was a Christian and wanted to wait for marriage to have sex. He understood my boundaries and still wanted to pursue me. We quickly started to date but I never asked him for anything. In the midst of being evicted, he called me while I was crying my eyes out. I told him about the situation and he was upset that I didn't tell him before. He told me to go find an apartment in New York and he would pay the security deposit and my first few months of rent.

Sounds like a great way out right? This was Egypt in disguise. I told him that I would call him back and I went into prayer. As I was spending time with the Lord, He told me that I run to relationships for comfort in the midst of pressure.

"Ok, Lord. You're so right. Now, what do I do?"

"Decline his offer and break up with him."

"WHAT?! Come on Lord, this could clearly be an answered prayer."

If only you could see my face in that moment. Not only am I evicted, I have nowhere to go, no money, and you want me to break up with my little boyfriend and decline his offer?

FINE.

I called him, broke things off and said thank you

but no thank you. He was pretty shocked to say the least. He felt like I was trying to be an "independent woman" when he was trying to help.

The Lord quickly gave me peace, "Do not put your trust in humans, for they are as frail as breath. (Isaiah 2:22)"

God was showing me under pressure that He is jealous for me. He wanted my attention. He wanted me to focus on Him and not my situation. He wanted all of me and most importantly, He wanted to rescue me from this test. When everything was ripped from under me I was exposed and needed saving by my Savior. I was in the most vulnerable place and that's where God does his work – when we reveal our need for him. I was finally growing in this area of trusting God! I no longer had a plan B! He was my plan A-Z. So, what happened to my homeless self?

God totally exceeded my expectations. A friend of my roommate heard about what happened and offered me a place to stay until I could get on my

31

feet. After about six months, we were able to afford a two-bedroom apartment in a high rise right outside of the city.

I wouldn't have been able to afford the places that my then boyfriend offered to pay for! I would have felt obligated to stay in the relationship under pressure to pay my rent. I would have been totally outside of God's will and in complete disobedience. Some of you have made decisions out of pressure and fear and now you feel stuck. Did you know that God wants to rescue you from even those situations that you put yourself in? Staying in that position is really up to us. It's a choice. I could have ignored God and called that man's offer an "answered prayer." It wasn't an answered prayer. It was a counterfeit. I later found out that I wasn't the only one he was dating, which explains why he was ok with not having sex with me. I didn't mind as much when I found out because I really didn't like him. He just filled a void that I hadn't surrendered to God yet.

Isn't it crazy how your standards change when you're under pressure or going through a test? In my right mind he wasn't my type at all. He wasn't anything I would want in a man or a husband but because I was in a lonely season, I grabbed onto what I could see.

In the midst of pressure my character was revealed. Sometimes we make permanent decisions based on temporary pressures, so what has the pressure you've been under revealed about who you are?

Let's look at a few examples:

Your Husband Recently Lost His Job

You work a 9-5 and you have two small children to take care of. You're feeling the pressure of not having two incomes and you don't feel like he's moving fast enough to get another job. You're thinking, "Does he not see all of these bills?" This is just a test. Ephesians 6:12 tells us, "For we are not fighting against flesh-and-blood enemies, but against evil rulers and authorities of the unseen world, against mighty powers in this dark world, and against evil spirits in the heavenly places."

It is Satan's goal to get you stressed out and weak under pressure. It's his goal for you to disrespect and undermine your husband. His goals are confusion and dissention. The issue is not your husband's work ethic or lack thereof, it's not his boss, *it's your response to the conflict.* You can yell and scream and put even more pressure on him or you can believe the best, pray like crazy, support, encourage and trust that God will provide for your family.

Do you know what else is amazing? God provided a job for you which means He provided a job for your household. I have learned that God blesses a cheerful giver. We typically use this scripture in church but it can also apply to your marriage. You are cheerfully giving to the needs of your household because you are thankful that God still made a way for some income to come into the house. It may not be enough in your mind but it may just mean that you get to be resourceful for a season until your husband is back on his feet. *God will reward you based on the way you treat him.* If you walk around with an attitude the amount you have been blessed with could very well be taken away from you. At times, we think of ourselves much higher than we ought to and God has a beautiful way of humbling us.

You Have No Financial Aid in School

It's your senior year and you are so ready to graduate but you're unable to finish your degree. How are you going to get the money? Are you going to put pressure on your parents to provide when you know they do not have it? Maybe you have cussed out financial aid a few times but things still haven't changed. The way you react to a situation you cannot control proves what is in your heart. It proves that you may struggle with patience, doubt, worry and rebellion. The image is crashing in your mind of the perfect "laid out" plans. Sit before the Lord. Get quiet. He may tell you to take a semester off to work and save until you can afford it again. Wait, what? That was not in the plans Heather. I want what I want NOW. Well maybe God is trying to develop your character and patience through this test. There is a bigger picture on the other side of all of this!

You're Single and Tired of It.

The pressure of being the only single friend in your group while you're pushing 30 is causing you to feel absolutely overwhelmed. You've joined every dating website and you spend most of your free time browsing profiles — searching for a husband. What does this tell you about your character?

You have a hard time trusting God's timing and the pressure around you causes you to make irrational decisions that are led by your flesh. There is nothing wrong with desiring marriage but we should never make a decision to pursue it because we are "tired of being single." I have met so many women that rush into marriage because they don't think that anybody else would want them. They have children and the marriage crumbles in a few years because she got married for the wrong reason – affecting a whole generation of children.

These are just a few examples but we could go on and on with examples of how God actually wants us to welcome difficult situations because it builds endurance.

Romans 5:3-6 says, "We gladly suffer, because we know that suffering helps us to endure. And endurance builds character, which gives us a hope that will never disappoint us. All of this happens because God has given us the Holy Spirit, who fills our hearts with his love. Christ died for us at a time when we were helpless and sinful."

I challenge you to get raw and naked before God in this season. I challenge you to let him shine a light in your heart so that you can truly see yourself and who you are. I saw who I was under pressure and I didn't like it. It didn't match up with what I was praying. I needed to change and it started with me truly surrendering everything to Jesus.

I know the seeds of being pressured have been planted in your heart from a very young age, but it must all change now. Today. You will be free right now in the name of Jesus.

> Out of my distress I called on the Lord; the Lord answered me and set me free. The Lord is on my side; I will not fear. What can man do to me? - Psalm 118:5-6

CHAPTER THREE
DISTRACTION PRESSURES

Let's talk about distractions. If you purchased this book months ago and you're just now picking it up — you may have been distracted. Haha, just kidding. I believe that God's timing is perfect and I am excited to meet you where you are with this book.

I recall a time when a few of my friends invited me to a Barre class. It was my first class and the instructor was nice enough to do the exercises next to us because we clearly didn't know what we were doing. The instructor got up and started to walk around. She began talking through the exercises but I couldn't see what she was doing. There was woman to my right that looked pretty confident. I started to just copy what she was doing because she looked like she had done this before. After copying her for a few minutes, it turns out that she didn't know what she was doing either! The instructor had to come over and correct me.

Isn't it ironic that when we can no longer hear God or maybe we don't understand what He is doing we start copying other people while thinking that if it's right for them it must be the same for us? Honey, God didn't tell you to start that thing. *You saw someone else do it and because you saw their success, you thought you could mimic the anointing.* You don't have to copy anybody else's gifts, talents, or ideas. God is big enough to give you your own witty ideas and inventions but are you willing to sit quietly at his feet to get the instructions?

I believe that distractions are one of the greatest attacks of the enemy. Distractions take the focus off of God and puts it on "self." Life becomes all about you – your struggles, your frustrations, your hurts, your pains.

Let's look at distractions defined:

- A thing that prevents someone from giving full attention to something else.
- Synonyms – diversions, interruptions, disturbance, interference and hindrance

What is causing you division, disturbance, or hindering your focus on what God instructed you to do?

The pressure we put on ourselves and the pressure we feel from outside sources is the ULTIMATE distraction to what God actually wants you to experience.

Do you know that it's Satan's desire to sift you like wheat?

> Simon, Simon, Satan has asked to sift each of you like wheat. But I have pleaded in prayer for you Simon, that your faith should not fail. So, when you have repented and turned to me again, strengthen your brothers. Luke 22:31-32

Sifting is a technique used in baking that refines the texture of flour or grain so that it is more delicate and easily manipulated when mixing with other ingredients.

Satan wants to refine your texture so that you can be swayed and blown in the way he desires to use you, as opposed to standing firm in the faith you have in God.

Imagine a huge wire mesh with holes shaped like faithless men and women. Satan aims to throw people into this mesh sleeve and shake them around all these jagged edges until they are thinned and worn down enough to fall into the holes of the faithless.

But faith cannot fall through the mesh. It's the wrong shape. It won't fit.

Anytime Satan tries to sift me it seems like I am being attacked in every area out of nowhere. Over time I have realized that I have a choice. Obviously, Satan had to ask God for permission to test me AND

God needed to use this to burn out some stuff that is in my heart that isn't like Him. Our focus during that sifting must be Jesus. It cannot be social media, our friends, a little boo, shopping or overeating. Satan seeks to distract you during this time in order to get you to give up your faith. Sifting.

When I think about the enemy sifting us, I think about the pressure of being "tossed" around in the midst of a test or trial. When you're getting tested, you may be tempted to find the easy way out because the pressure is so intense. It's dangerous if you begin to look at yourself versus keeping your eyes on Jesus. The pressure that comes from sifting is only a distraction to get you to give up your faith. Don't ever give in to him! Ever.

As long as you hold onto your faith and trust in the power and the goodness of God, then your faith will keep you in the texture God intended for you.

What are some areas where Satan will try to sift you?

Attacks Against Your Marriage or Family

If you are firm in your faith, I have learned that the enemy will try to come for your family or people close to you who aren't as established in their faith. But I understand that this fight is spiritual (Ephesians 6:12) so I fight by faith alone. This area can be difficult because you expect your spouse and family to be your biggest supporters and confidants, but they can also be used as a pathway for Satan to have access to you. Ask the Holy Spirit to reveal the distractions that take form in the shape of your loved ones and how to stay focused on what is important.

Finances

When you get attacked in your finances it is easy to abandon your faith by focusing on your physical lack instead of on the power of God. Difficult times are allowed so that they transform us and reveal our need for God. I needed to be really broke for a season so I could learn how to manage 50 cents. I can laugh about it now but I was unfaithful and God HAD to strip me in this area because my mindset was wrong. I was in debt and I was spending money I didn't have on credit cards I barely paid. If you feel like you're unfaithful in this area and you're not sure what to do – ask the Lord to give you wisdom and to change your perspective about the difficulties you're enduring. (James 1:5)

Attacks Against Your Mind

Have you ever felt like a failure and like you have no reason to live? I have felt that way before. More recently, my husband went through a very difficult time where he felt he had no reason to live. He had been a pastor for 5 years, we had been married for six, and had two children at that time. It can truly happen to anyone. Satan was preying on his insecurities and trying to convince him with his own thoughts that he wasn't a good enough husband, father, or pastor. I was so proud when he broke free from those thoughts by using the word of God to speak over himself. He could listen to God's word or the enemies lies. He made a decision to grow and pass that test.

Infertility, Pregnancy and Miscarriage

As women, we are constantly pressured about our bodies. The toll pregnancy has on a woman's body is a huge physical battle, yet it is often minimized as if it is just a given that we will not only get pregnant but have no complications along the way. So when we do face tough times in this area, it can cause us to lose sight of the fact that God is faithful. This type of distraction can be especially trying because we truly have no say over when and under what circumstances God opens our womb. But it does allow for God to be God and the opportunity for us to truly trust him while he stretches our faith.

Singleness

Satan may be suggesting crazy thoughts to you about your singleness: "You will be single your entire life." "You need to compromise in order to get a man." "You need to dress a certain way if you want to be noticed." Don't entertain his lies and stop talking to a fallen angel. He's a liar. There's NEVER any truth in him. Satan preys on the things we are most insecure about. He preys on our thoughts and is constantly looking for a way to keep us weak so that he can keep us far from God. If you are single, this is the time to put on the full armor of God. Do not get distracted by what you think you want.

There could be a million areas where Satan tries to attack and "sift" you like wheat. But this is why we must stay on guard with the word of God in our hearts so you can overcome his schemes. Start fighting back. Satan is after your faith.

We know that Hebrews 11:6 tells us that it's impossible to please God without faith.

2 Corinthians 10:5 tells us to capture every thought and make it submit to Jesus Christ.

1 Samuel 30:6 reminds us that David was greatly distressed because his soldiers wanted to kill him but he stirred himself up in the Lord and was strengthened in Him.

Romans 8:25 tells us that all things work together for the good of those who love Him.

If you don't have the word of God hidden in your heart, then it won't come out of you when you're being pressured in life. It is a given that you will be pressured in every season. It's not a matter of *if* but *when.* Will you let it distract you from your faith or will you guard your heart with God's word?

Let's read Luke 10:38 – 42:

> As Jesus and the disciples continued on their way to Jerusalem, they came to a certain village where a woman named Martha welcomed Him into her home. Her sister, Mary, sat at the Lord's feet, listening to what he taught. But Martha was *distracted* by the big dinner she was

48

preparing. She came to Jesus and said, 'Lord, doesn't it seem unfair to you that my sister just sits here while I do all the work? Tell her to come and help me.'

But the Lord said to her, 'My dear Martha, you are worried and upset over all these details! There is only one thing worth being concerned about. Mary has discovered it, and it will not be taken away from her.'"

Martha was concerned with her own thoughts of what was important instead of acknowledging Jesus. Have you ever been distracted by your thoughts?

- Lord, it's unfair that my life turned out this way and so and so's life turned out so much better.
- Isn't it unfair Lord that my marriage is falling apart and this other woman is happy in her marriage and she didn't even do it God's way!
- Isn't it unfair that I have been single for seven years and sister so and so just came

to the church last week, just got saved and she already has her man?

- Isn't it unfair that I have been serving in ministry for years and so and so just got promoted?
- Isn't it unfair that I am still not the manager but I do all of the work?

Martha invited Jesus in but Mary was sitting at his feet. *This is proof that we can invite Jesus into our home but not into our heart.* Martha was distracted with how her home appeared to Jesus when He was only concerned with her faith and what was on the inside of her.

I have definitely felt like Martha. When my husband and I stepped out into ministry full time I just assumed that things would explode really fast and people would just show up to our bible studies and events. Definitely not. It's safe to say that the journey has been slow and steady. When you come from a big ministry, you don't understand the time and cost it takes to build one. My goal went from having a big ministry to helping whoever would listen.

There is a stigma in our society that if it's not "huge," it's not successful and that is far from the truth. If your bible study only has five women until Jesus returns, you poured into those five people and they poured into ten more and so on. Each soul matters. Each person matters. Don't be distracted by what you think it should look like – be focused on the role God gave you where you are.

Let's remove the word "unfair" from our vocabulary and replace it with, "Isn't God faithful?" Let's go from rushing around with the details to sitting at the feet of the Father.

If I can be honest, I can be a little "type A" with my time with Jesus. I pray, spend time with Jesus, journal and talk to Him. This is all good but I came to a point in my walk where I was very much like

Martha in my quiet time. I was more about routine and less about a heart to spend time with God. I remember a time when I was waiting for the Lord to give me a sermon title. I went to the Lord every day that week, "COME ON JESUS. GIVE ME A SERMON." You KNOW I am going to be preaching in front of thousands of people. It would be nice if you gave me a sermon. I was just two days away from preaching and I sat defeated in my prayer room. "Lord, I know you have called me to this. Why isn't it clear?

He said to me:

> *"I don't want you to come to me just to get the answer concerning your life Heather. I want you to spend time with me because you love me and because you know I enjoy spending time with you too. Nobody wants to feel like you're only going to them just to get an answer. I am not playing a cruel game with you. I want your heart my child. I want you. Through fellowship with me, I will show you the way. I want you to come deeper with me.*

Yes, you're doing all of these things for me but if you aren't careful, you will do them out of routine and not love. Slow down. Come and sit with me with no agenda. I want your heart."

TALK ABOUT WRECKED. I probably cried for 30 minutes after He said this to me. I went to Jesus as a mark on my "to do" list. It escaped my mind that He actually wanted to spend time with me. The Holy Spirit wanted me. Just me. Now I enter my quiet time a bit calmer. Less structure, less "needing an answer," and more LOVE. It's because I love my Jesus that I get to spend time with Him.

Have you gotten so busy and distracted in your life that your service to God is due to routine? And trust me, I am a mom of two with one on the way – the pressure to get distracted is real. I feel like I'm juggling at times, while dropping balls in between. But, I always run back and cling to my faith in Jesus Christ as my foundation.

Don't beat yourself up if you don't have it all together. NOBODY has it all together. It's all an illusion. There is enough pressure put on us from outsiders but many times we put pressure on OURSELVES to be perfect. Just stop it. Work out your own salvation (Philippians 2:12) and stay focused on what the Lord is specifically telling you to do. So you don't get the dishes done for a couple of days – it's not the end of the world. Go spend time with your kids, dance and laugh with them. Stop being so pressured and stressed out. You are welcoming those spirits right into your family. Your children will walk around feeling that same stress.

The weapons of our warfare are not carnal, but SPIRITUAL. (2 Corinthians 10:4) We must not fight supernatural battles with our flesh. Let's do something different. Let's fight back spiritually.

CHAPTER FOUR
APPROVAL ADDICTION

One of the reasons that people get caught in the trap of being pressured is because they are concerned with gaining the approval of others. They want people to approve of them. From family members, to old classmates, to colleagues, even strangers. Some of us want to create the perfect social media life to satisfy our addiction to approval.

John 5:41-44 says, "Your approval means nothing to me, because I know you don't have God's love within you. For I have come to you in my Father's name, and you have rejected me. Yet if others come in their own name, you gladly welcome them. No wonder you can't believe! For you gladly honor each other, but you don't care about the honor that comes from the one who alone is God."

Jesus wasn't after the approval of people that didn't have God's love in them. He only sought to please God so their worldly opinions didn't matter. No matter what they said about Jesus, He knew they would never understand Him because they rejected His way of living and thinking. The Jewish leaders also scrutinized everything Jesus did. "Why did you heal on the Sabbath? Why do you call yourself one with God, why do you do this or that?" Jesus could do nothing right in their eyes. They were critical, rude, and harsh towards Him. These Jewish elders asked Pontius Pilate to judge and condemn Jesus, accusing him of claiming to be the King of the Jews and plotted to kill Him. Jesus knew why he was sent to the earth. He wasn't trying to be flashy or doing miracles just for show. In John 7, Jesus stayed in Galilee and didn't want to go to Judea because the Jewish leaders were looking for a way to kill him. The

Jewish Festival of Tabernacles was coming up and Jesus' brothers said to him, "Leave Galilee and go to Judea so that your disciples may see the works that you do. (John 7:3)" They told Jesus "Nobody who wants to become a public figure acts in secret. Since you are doing these things, show yourself to the world."

Jesus's own brothers didn't believe in him. They didn't believe that he was the Messiah and suggested he show himself so that they and others could approve of him. What did Jesus do after he was pressured by his brothers? Did he just go to the Festival to gain their approval? No. He told them in John 7:6 that it wasn't his time yet and to go without him.

Jesus KNEW who he was, WHOSE he was, and WHY he was sent to this earth. He didn't need the Jewish leader's approval and he definitely didn't need his own brothers to approve of him. Because his brothers grew up with him, he was just "Jesus," to them. Ever had that happen to you? Oh, that's just so and so? It's that spirit of familiarity that causes people to not believe in you. The enemy uses that spirit to attack you to make you feel like you didn't hear God correctly. Maybe people ignore your gifts and talents and tell you what you cannot do. Maybe they knew you before you knew Christ, when you "used to be" someone else. Maybe someone wrote you off and said that you will never be successful and since then, that nagging voice has tormented you. You put more hope in that voice than you do in the voice of the Holy Spirit. When things don't work out you begin to think in your flesh, "They're right. I am not made for this. I will never be who God called me to be."

I came to say that the devil IS A LIAR. Because Jesus knew who he was, he didn't need approval from anyone else. He stayed put in Galilee because he didn't need to go and prove himself to anybody. He didn't need to do anything "extra." He knew that he walked in the authority of God. He knew who sent him. And guess what? When you confess that Jesus is Lord of your life, you now have a blood-bought right through Jesus to come boldly to the throne of God as his own CHILD (Hebrews 4:16).

The approval of the Jewish leaders meant NOTHING to Jesus because his identity was in the one who sent him.

What does that tell me about your life? It tells me that when people hate you, talk about you, or make up things about you, their approval shouldn't matter either. Who are they again? Your family? Strangers? Your boss? Do they belong to Christ? Do they have your best interest? Are they truly led by the Holy Spirit? Do they confirm what the Holy Spirit has shown you first?

I have a SMALL pocket of accountability that corrects and rebukes me because they know me; I walk with them in life and I know they are filled with Christ's love. Whoever is speaking into your life needs to be filled with God's love. If that person is not filled with God's love, then why are you taking instructions from them? I truly believe that we should honor our parents but if our parents are telling us to do something that contradicts God's word then we need to obey the one who created us.

I've learned that a person can say they love God but that doesn't mean they do or that they are truly committed to living for him. A tree is identified by its fruit. If a tree is bad, its fruit will be bad (Matthew 12:33). If you say that you love Jesus, there will be fruit in your life of that love. How will you know if what someone says is bathed in God's love? It will convict you to do the right thing, even though your flesh wants to do something else.

Now that you recognize that your identity is in Jesus Christ, how do we get free from this approval addiction? The need to be liked and affirmed?

First, it's natural to want to be loved. I believe that God made us that way but with the fall of Adam and

Eve in the garden, sin came and Satan has been attacking people's identities since that day. "Did God really say..." is one of his number one lies.

I want to look at a few steps to be free from approval addiction:

1. The first step to this freedom is to recognize that Jesus died for you on the cross so that you may be reconciled with him forever. Jesus made a BLOOD covenant with us where he laid down his life for me and you. We are under the covering of Jesus Christ. Before we were even born, God already had a plan for you. While you were in your mother's womb, God already had a plan assigned for you. (Jeremiah 1:5)

2. The second step is to recognize that the key to getting free in a certain area is to finally pass the test when it comes around. So yes, as you declare that you are free, cry at the altar, and repent, that same test will repeat itself in your

life because Satan knows it to be a weak area for you. Do you think he is going to sit there and let you just skip off in the wind with your freedom? No, your faith is going to be TESTED. In order to get FREE from approval addiction, you will find that people are talking about you, bashing you, disagreeing with you, being rude towards you or whatever else. But what are you going to do different in order to pass the test of disapproval? When the test comes, pass it. There needs to be rest in your spirit by overcoming evil with good. Don't clap back. Decide that you won't care what they think about you because your approval comes from Christ alone.

3. Recognize that this fight is spiritual, not physical. If Satan can use approval addiction to distract you, he will. He watches and studies your every move. Stop running from the process and use this opportunity as a time to

grow. People always ask me, "Heather how do you do it all with so many people critiquing you?" I have truly learned to silence the millions of voices in order to press forward to do what God has called me to do. How did this happen? I recognized that Satan wants to distract me and he will use people to do it. I must guard my heart against the desire to gain the approval of people.

Years ago, a leader at a church I attended made up a really bad rumor about me. They spread this rumor to the men's ministry and began making up terrible things about me. Here I am, serving and living for Jesus when I get a call from the church asking me to come in to meet with leadership. One of the leaders shows me a photo of a woman who is pretty much naked but covering her face and breasts with her arms and hands. She had a six pack and some fabulous hips.

I thought, "Now, why would you show me a picture of some naked woman? I don't want to see that mess!"

"Heather, is this you?"

I literally laughed. In that moment I wasn't mad but I laughed because there was no way that they could be serious, right? Of COURSE, that wasn't me. I was in disbelief. I mean, physically she isn't me. I don't have any hips and I don't have a six pack. More like a 4 pack. ☺

After the initial shock, I had a choice in that moment. Am I going to forgive or am I going to hold onto the hurt I felt at the hands of these people? Prior to this, I had been praying to be free from people bondage. Praying that I didn't need the approval of others in order to feel valued. Praying that God would show me that I was enough. Right in the midst of my crying out to God, this horrific test was thrown in my path.

Immediately, the Holy Spirit showed me that this was a test, a test that I can choose to pass. Either I will get wrapped up in the empty words of this "leader" or I will forgive, move on and not try to prove myself to anyone. I forgave that leader immediately. I passed the test! It felt so good to not be in bondage to what those guys thought about me. The crazy thing is, right when my husband and I met – those same leaders tried to convince him not to talk to me. I laughed it off because I knew who I was in Jesus Christ. I know who I am and your words cannot stop God's plan for me.

Sadly, they are still stagnant in their life. How can God grow your ministry, your life and take you into what He has called you to do if you are too busy tearing everyone down? You will not harvest publicly if your goal is to privately tear down everyone. I pray that they will truly change and maybe they have but I am not the judge of hearts.

Nonetheless, your focus cannot be on other

people if you are going to do what God has called you to do. IF you have that much time on your hands, use that energy to bring glory to God. Stop meddling. Don't talk about people. Don't gossip. Don't complain. Don't make up rumors.

God showed me that that little rumor was nothing compared to what He was preparing me for. I NEEDED to be free from people. I needed to strengthen that "muscle." How do you expect to grow your freedom from people bondage "muscle" if you aren't exercising it? You have to put some more weight or pressure on it in order for it to grow. Seeking the approval of others will keep us trapped under the pressure to conform to other people's ideas for us. It was just that small rumor for me but it could be something else the next day. If I spend my entire life sitting at the feet of a bunch of people that don't have the love of Jesus in their hearts, then there is no way that I could do what I am doing today.

Now, you may be reading this and think, "but I took some naked photos." Honey, the blood of Jesus can cover that too. When we repent of our sins, God is faithful and just to forgive us and to cleanse us of all unrighteousness. (1 John 1:9) I love to share my messy past because it shows others that if God can save and deliver me, He can save and deliver you too.

When I think about the freedom that I now walk in to do what God has called me to do, I look at it like there is a million voices screaming at me but I am only tuned into One. The Holy Spirit. He shows me which way to go, He leads and guides me by His spirit, He comforts and convicts me. He also sends the right people around me to correct me. I no longer walk in that bondage and it was a journey of caring less about what people thought of me. I'm not moved by money, power, status, likes or anything else. I am truly at peace because I know that everyone may not understand me but if I stay connected to the One who saved my soul, I will be ok.

Don't get caught up in trying to get people to like you or understand your standards in Christ. Just keep living for Him. A changed life speaks volumes more than words can.

I don't know about you – but I want to stand before Jesus one day and hear Him say, "well done, my good and faithful servant. You have run the race well."

CHAPTER FIVE

SOCIAL MEDIA/DIGITAL PRESSURE

Ah, good ol' social media.

Social media used to be a place where you could connect with people you went to school with or give small updates to how you were thinking or feeling on a particular day. It has now become a catalyst to a major shift in our generation! I am so thankful that it wasn't around when I was making some really bad decisions in high school and college.

The only record you all have is what I choose to tell you. For this next generation, everything from their past will be recorded, screenshotted, snap-chatted and on the internet forever. It's becoming more and more obvious how the pressure of social media is affecting self-perception in teenage girls AND adult women. I can see it all around me. Pressure to be perfect and have it all together. Pressure to have a perfect life with perfect travels. To look perfect, act perfect, have the perfect body, have the perfect group of friends, the perfect amount of likes on Instagram. Perfect, perfect, perfect. And if you don't meet these ridiculously high standards then the self-loathing and bullying begins. It seems like every time we turn around there is new story of a 12-year-old committing suicide because she or he was bullied online.

But let's just be honest, social media has become an avenue by which our insecurities and self-loathing are materialized. It gives a voice to the negativity we may be experiencing internally.

I want you to stop for a moment and ask yourself these questions:

- What pressures do we feel as a result of scrolling through someone's timeline?
- What traps of comparison are we caught in when we idolize the lives of others?

When you scroll through your timelines, you may feel a huge range of highs and lows. You aren't warned if a person's status is messy, cursing and drama filled, or if it will cause you to stumble in your faith. You go from anger to joy to jealousy in a matter of 20 seconds and it's exhausting. Then you see someone doing really well in their life and naturally compare it to where you are in life. Inferiority has planted its seed but you keep on scrolling. When you look up two weeks later, you don't feel like you're enough but you don't know why.

You begin to question your job, where you live, and you start to search for "better" to make up for that "enough" feeling. That seed continues to be watered by your thoughts. What a waste of time! It's a TRAP to get you focused on the lives of others. Your grass is as green as you have decided to water it.

On the other hand, Social media can be a tremendous blessing. It's not always "bad." The thing is, sex isn't "bad." Sex is only bad outside of marriage. Sex is an amazing gift from God when you're married as it brings you closer to your spouse, but your motive and mindset determine the effect that things have on your life. Why are you online? To connect with old friends, keep up with new ones, to promote your business, to share Jesus? With all things you should have purpose in what you consume or share because if you aren't careful, you can silently make an idol out of social media.

What is an idol? An idol is anything that takes the place of God in your heart. Maybe you check your phone a zillion times a day, maybe your heart gets crushed if you share an encouraging post but nobody likes or comments. Maybe you take a million pictures of one outfit but nothing seems to work out. You've spent one hour trying to get the perfect photo but you haven't spent an hour with God in months. You say, "I don't have time to spend with God," but you do have time to scroll through social media at night.

Imagine this – you had a standing lunch date every single day with someone you really admire. It could be a past president, preacher, or anyone you would want to learn from. You would sit there and soak in every single word. You wouldn't dare pick up the phone and talk to a friend. You wouldn't dare scroll through social media. Why? Because that person carries value to you. Well the most revered person on this entire earth still doesn't compare to Jesus Christ and what he did for you. He sent HIS spirit to this earth to LIVE in you. The Holy Spirit is living in you and sitting in your room every single day, waiting for you to come and spend time with him.

You're rushing around doing all of these things just to share them on social media while you're literally forgetting about him. We are no longer bowing down and worshipping Baal or created gold statues but we are bowing down and worshipping Instagram, Snapchat, Facebook and Twitter. We say things like, "I don't feel close to God," or "God doesn't speak to me," but God is always speaking. You're just heavily distracted and don't have ears to hear. Can God speak through the clutter? Do you get quiet enough to hear His voice?

So, what is distracting you? Is it TV? Internet? What external things are fulfilling the time you would typically spend with the Lord?

According to a 2012 study posted on the National Institutes of health website, "Internet Addiction Disorder (IAD) ruins lives by causing neurological complications, psychological disturbances, and social problems." It is still not officially listed as a psychiatric disorder in the bible of psychiatric disease, the Diagnostic and Statistical Manual of Mental Disorders (DSM-V), though the more narrowly defined Internet Gaming Addiction was added in May 2013.

Other subtypes of Internet addiction -- such as social media addiction -- have not been studied enough to receive their own clinical definitions or treatment recommendations. But some of the research on Internet addiction in general may shed light on the observations about social media.

Symptoms for Internet addiction can be similar to addiction to anything else and fall into two types of behaviors: an ever increasing need to engage with the object of the addiction, and a bad feeling when not getting enough of it. Psychiatrist and neuroscience researcher Sean Luo of Columbia University says an internet user worried that their online use is getting out of control should seek a professional evaluation. "It is not so much the particular behaviors" that lead to a diagnosis of inappropriate Internet use or addiction, he said, but "the severity, the functional status of the patient" and whether their behaviors "interfere with school, work, or social activities."

Do you feel like you need to engage with people constantly, post photos for attention, comments and likes? We all post and like to interact with people but is it consuming you? If you don't get enough likes or comments, does it ruin your day? Do you feel less pretty or like you aren't good enough based on your interactions online? Do you subconsciously base your worth and value on if people like your posts or not? If any of these are true for you, you should evaluate how much time you are spending on social media and how it is contributing to your closeness or distance from God. As noted before, anything that we put before our relationship with God is an idol and should be eliminated from our lives until we are disciplined enough to set healthy boundaries.

Let's keep reading the study:

A boy who was addicted to the internet has his brain scanned for research purposes at Daxing

Internet Addiction Treatment Center in Beijing February 22, 2014. (Source: REUTERS/KIM KYUNG-HOON)

According to several recent brain imagining studies, severely affected Internet addicts show structural and functional brain abnormalities similar to those found in people with substance abuse problems. Other research has shown that Internet addiction frequently coexists with anxiety, depression, or an addiction to other things like alcohol or drugs.

A blog post by social media marketer Jason Thibeault, "Why I just quit Facebook," is sparking new debate about the risks of social media addiction. Why did Thibault find Facebook, in particular, so addictive? He writes that it's because "we are essentially narcissistic and want to be the center of attention.... I want them to pay attention to me, to 'like' me, that's why."

Ironically, some aspects of social media activity

(for example, getting "likes") appear to stimulate reward centers in the brain.

While Thibault's solution -- quitting cold turkey -- may work for him, Luo says it's not for everyone. (And it's worth noting that while Thibault quit Facebook, he remains active on LinkedIn, Twitter and other social media sites.)

According to Luo, "cold turkey might work for some, but others may need more help." He says there are "no FDA approved medications, and no randomized trials published for medications to treat Internet addiction."

Thibeault wrote that he quit Facebook because "my news feeds were becoming an addiction. They were a constant interruption pulling me away from the work that I was otherwise enjoying."

"Just imagine that Facebook is like a digital water cooler. I was drinking A TON of water every hour," he wrote. "Although I'm not a neuroscientist, I'd venture to say that what was happening was related to my Dopamine levels--when I was checking status updates on Facebook, my brain was rewarding itself with Dopamine; when I wasn't, and Dopamine levels dropped as a result, I started 'jonesing for a fix.'"

"So I quit," he wrote. "Cold turkey."

Isn't this study mind blowing? What happens when you tell your flesh "no" to social media? It's a good sign that social media may have a control on you. Now, I am even convicted in writing this chapter. I believe that I have a healthy mindset towards social media. I don't place my value or worth in it because I understand that it is an avenue where I can share Jesus. But, I do have my phone a lot. Even as I write this – I at times feel the need to pick up my phone and check my email and text messages. I literally have to tell myself: NO PHONE HEATHER. You are busy. I also do no TV, no kids right now. (Hey, I need to be able to focus and work) So, when I feel that dopamine level drop, I remind its tail that it doesn't control me. Social media doesn't control me. My current 76,193 unread emails don't control me (insert tears. Yes, that's the real unread number.)

I love these scriptures about disciplining your flesh and refusing to procrastinate:

> Whatever you find to do with your hands, do it with all your might, because there is neither work nor planning nor knowledge nor wisdom in the grave, the place where you will eventually go. Ecclesiastes 9:10

> Whatever you do, do it enthusiastically, as something done for the Lord and not for men. Colossians 3:23

> Do not be slothful in zeal, be fervent in spirit, serve the Lord. Romans 12:11

> LORD, remind me how brief my time on earth will be. Remind me that my days are numbered—how fleeting my life is. You have made my life no longer than the width of my hand. My entire lifetime is just a moment to you; at best, each of us is but a breath. Psalm 39:4-5

These scriptures remind me that whatever I am working on, I should do it enthusiastically and as unto the Lord. It tells me that I need to be faithful and disciplined in how I approach my calling and this includes setting boundaries with social media. It tells me that I don't have a ton of time on this earth and I don't want to waste it online, looking for approval. It tells me that I shouldn't waste my days being lazy or doing anything that doesn't contribute to what God has called me to.

I truly believe that God wants me on social media. He wants to use it as a tool to further spread the gospel of Jesus. He doesn't want me on there gossiping, meddling, and showing my breasts. He wants me to reach people with the gospel that I may not have otherwise encountered. And of course, show some cute pictures of my hubby and kids! If you're reading this and you're finding that you're having an issue with social media being a distraction to your walk with God, set some boundaries. There are apps for your phone that actually track your screen time. I really like the "Moment" app. I just have the regular version, not the upgraded version. This app actually tracks your screen time and how much you spend on certain apps. It's a great way to get convicted to see how much time you wasted on your phone. I am a numbers person. If I can see how much time I wasted (once it was like 2 hours 2 minutes on my phone) I was kind of mad. I'm like Heather, get your life together. You're on a time limit. Imagine if someone decreased their screen time by an average of 1 hour and 2 minutes per day? That's 377 HOURS a year. You just gave yourself a ton of extra time. This means that you have an extra 15.7 DAYS to do something. Whew.

You see, the reason why I really wanted you to hear about the study and read those scriptures is because I want you to understand that when your value, worth and identity are in these things then you will allow social media to pressure you to start something that God never told you to start. This is a great way to get convicted of how much time you've devoted to something that is either feeding you or draining you.

I find that social media is a breeding ground for the enemy to prey on people who may be struggling with the sin of comparison or who are not confident in the season they are in. If you see lots of engagements around December or February, then you may look at your single season as a punishment. If you are believing God for children, you may get discouraged by the number of people getting pregnant while you can't understand why it hasn't happened for you yet.

If you're a wife constantly fighting with your spouse, then see a husband or a wife profess their undying love for each other on social media, you may think, "I sure don't feel that way about my spouse." Or, "I wish my husband would say those nice things about me. It's just not fair. I married the wrong one." Wait, yesterday you loved him and you were obsessed with him. So, today you guys are fighting and you wish he was like some other man?? You mean the man that you prayed for? The one that fathers your children? The one you do life with? Did you really just let somebody else's life belittle the one you have built?? Again, if you're fighting with your guy – get off social media for a few hours. You're full of "the fight" and you may subliminally post things to further upset him and add fuel to a pretty bad fire already. Social media is great but it should NEVER ruin your relationships, especially the one with your man.

What if you're a mother and you see a child saying his "ABC's" and he is under 1? You may wonder – why doesn't my kid know their ABC's? My kids is like 15 months. Why is my child so slow? Am I not a good parent? Maybe, I should read more and work with them more." So then, you begin to question your parenting and compare the speech of one child against yours.

Again, a waste of time. Your child is perfect for

you. Yes, feel challenged to spend more time with your baby but don't start transferring that pressure onto your kid to know everything because you heard some other kid do something. I truly believe that our kids pick up on the "pressures" we put on them and others. I don't know about you but I want to pass on a legacy of a great Christian, wife and mother. Not one where I stressed my kids out.

Imagine this, you are online and you see that someone received a promotion or got accepted into a really good school. You on the other hand, received a denial letter. Now you feel like a total failure and instead of running to the feet of the Lord, you assume that God hates you. On the contrary, God does not hate you, He is simply protecting you from what you think you need in order to be satisfied. Instead, thank God for open and closed doors.

I recall a door that the Lord told me to close with a prominent woman preacher. The Lord made it clear that He wanted me to naturally separate myself from her. I had no peace with our relationship. The "me" side of life wants to be best friends forever with everyone. I want us all to skip off in the wind and all love Jesus forever without any jealousy, fear or stress. But, God was protecting the anointing on my life. He didn't want me to be influenced by her in anyway by her because she is older than me. I could have looked at it like, "woe is me. Lord, I prayed for more women to surround me in ministry but you just keep closing doors." I don't know about you but I have gone around that mountain. Instead, I'm like – "LORD, let thy will be done in my life. If you are giving me a check in my spirit, I need to listen. I trust your leading and guiding." So, if you are getting job doors or university doors slammed in your face, thank God. God is leading you in another direction. Praise God!

Distractions shift your focus from what God is developing in you to your own desires and emotions. Do not give distractions the power to pressure you.

Don't be mistaken, just because you don't have what you think you deserve or what everyone else has – God STILL loves you. Be mindful that Satan wants you to believe his lies and if we aren't careful about how we use social media, similar thoughts can create pressure within ourselves that we were never meant to carry.

I want you to know that "Digital Pressure" is real and Satan is seeking to destroy us by any means. If you feel that you are weak in some areas and find that you experience negative feelings scrolling through your timeline, take a break. If you find that you feel negatively about a person you follow, unfollow that person. Temptation lives on those timelines and we are called to do away with anything that causes us to stumble on our walk with Jesus.

As I wrap up this chapter, I want to challenge your own heart. Have you ever created a fake profile to bash someone? It's a sure sign that you need a nice break away from social media. How do you have time to create fake profiles to "tell people how you feel?"

What does the bible say about it?

> If another believer sins against you, go privately and point out the offense. If the other person listens and confesses it, you have won that person back.
> Matthew 18:15

Does it say, "If another believer sins against you, bash them publicly, create fake profiles and tear them apart?" You may be thinking, "well, I don't know them personally." Then you cannot hate someone you don't know. You don't KNOW them. Do you love EVERYTHING that all of your loved ones do? Of course you don't. Nobody 100% loves what a person does. So, if you cannot reach them, pray for them. Like really, really pray for them.

Matthew 12:36 says: And I tell you this, you must give an account on judgment day for every idle word you speak."

Whoa. This tells me that we will be judged on every single thing we say, think and even the words we write. So yes, every single status, comment and "dislike" will be judged. If I can keep it real with you – I want to encourage you with this: Don't be a hater. Like really. I don't even like the word "hater" but some people truly just hate on whatever everybody else does because they aren't satisfied or happy with their own life. Trying to blow somebody else's candle out won't make yours shine any brighter.

My prayer is that you will think eternally.

Colossians 3:2 tells us to set our mind on the things of heaven and not on earthly things. Don't get so caught up in this earth that you forget that there's an entire heaven and hell. Whenever I get focused on earthly things the Lord reminds me to adjust and then he challenges my prayers. I was standing in my prayer room and praying to the Lord when he asked me this question, "What do you want, Heather?"

Wait, huh? Is this a test Lord? Why are you asking me this question?

Then I heard it again, "Heather, what do you

want?"

So, I started to name a list of things that I would want.

I heard this in my spirit, "That's all?"

Wait, that's all, Lord? What do you mean, that's all? Then, I heard the Lord tell me, "Ask me for more of this particular thing."

Modestly, I increased it, feeling bad for even asking. Then I heard the Holy Spirit say to me, "Heather, you pray too small. I am trying to expand your mindset and your territory but your prayers are so small. I want you to start praying big prayers." That day, with the right heart, I wrote out my big prayers on a notepad. I wrote out things that I would be afraid to pray. I wrote out things that I would never share with anyone else in fear of what people may think of me. I wrote out things that were BIG in my heart – things I would only dream about. I realized that I needed to put a voice to those things that I wanted. I was getting caught up in worldly concerns without even realizing it. I was spending so much time on social media that my focus was no longer on eternal things. I didn't realize it but I lost sight of how magnificent God is by looking at the small daily aspirations on my timeline.

Satan comes in to cause distractions. One of his greatest weapons is to get you focused on what you can see over what God can do in your life. I love this line from "Clear the Stage" by Jeremy Needham: "Tell your friends that this is where the story ends unless you're broken for your sins you cannot be social."

That includes social media. Take a break if you need to. Take a break if you've stopped praying big because you're discontent and focused on what others are doing. Electronics should not have that much influence on you. Be free from that pressure.

CHAPTER SIX

PRESSURE IN MARRIAGE

Can I keep it real? Ok, so I used to pressure my husband a lot. When I first got married, I tried to pressure my husband to plan our dates and family trips. I quickly realized that my husband isn't a big planner when it comes to our date days or our family trips. At first, it frustrated me, until the Lord showed me that I was placing an expectation on my husband that He already fulfilled in me. God was using me to meet that need in our marriage and I was trying to get my husband to meet that need. We are one flesh, so if I'm good at it — then I eliminate that weakness in my husband and vice versa. I love to plan and organize and it's truly a gift. I do a lot of research and I am always able to find great deals that save us a lot of money on our trips. (see my blog, "How to travel the world for free ☺ www.heatherllindsey.com) Nonetheless, I would always tease my husband about our date days and say, "aww, I cannot wait for Friday! I just know that you planned THEE most romantic day." And, my husband would look at me like a deer in headlights. I now laugh it off because I have learned that him not being a planner didn't make him love me any less. Now, I have watched my husband grow in this area. Recently for date day, he scheduled a full day of couples facials and a trip to my favorite vegan restaurant. I had been wanting a facial for a while but I didn't say anything. This may seem small to someone else but it's proof that your man can grow in your marriage. Putting pressure on your spouse to change in a certain area when you're stronger isn't healthy for your marriage. Instead, give your expectations to the Lord. Stop pressuring him to do this or that and start thanking God for what he does bring to the table of your marriage. So, as I was writing this book, I figured that I wasn't the only woman pressuring her man about small and big things. I figured it would be perfect to include my husband's perspective in this book. Here you go- from my favorite human ever, Cornelius Lindsey.

***

My wife approached me with the idea of writing a chapter in this book about the pressure men feel from women. The relationship that best depicts this pressure is marriage.

Like most men, I love hanging out with my friends. As a married man, most of my friends are married, which means we have a lot of talks about marriage. While talking to my wife about her expectations for this chapter, she stressed to me the importance of sharing some of the things my friends and I have discussed about the pressure we felt our wives put on us.

The truth is we don't talk much about pressure in marriage for a couple of reasons. First, many of us believe that talking about the pressure can translate as weakness. Secondly, many of us feel that a certain degree of pressure is normal; therefore, we don't challenge it but learn to live with it. Thirdly, and you might be shocked to read this, but most of our pressure doesn't come from our wives, it comes from ourselves. Lastly, many men are too prideful to admit this and too intimidated to acknowledge it, but it is tough being a man.

From the time we are little boys, we're told to be strong. We are sent outside to play and to explore the curiosity of our minds. We get our hands dirty, jump off cliffs, play fight with sticks and imaginary enemies, wrestle other boys, and run until we get tired. When we get hurt, we're told to walk it off. When we're on the losing end of a game, we're told to get better so we can win next time. When we're falling behind, we're told that we need to lead. When we're feeling weak, we're told to be strong. That's pressure! From a young age, we are given high expectations that seem almost impossible to reach, especially when a father isn't present to lead the way. Instead of verbalizing our frustration with such high expectations, we repress it. We refuse to talk about it because it makes you appear weak and a man always wants to avoid appearing weak.

As Christians, we know that weakness is a true sign of strength. In fact, it was Apostle Paul who wrote in 2 Corinthians 12:10, "For when I am weak, then I am strong." We can conclude that true strength lies in the power of Christ, not the ability of man. However, our pride leads us to depend on ourselves, not Christ. Wherever pride abounds, weakness flourishes. Men choose weakness over strength because many of us believe that not talking about the pressure we feel means that it isn't truly affecting us. We try to convince ourselves that everything is okay and doesn't need to be talked about in depth. Our conversations amongst each other become very shallow and non-descriptive to avoid expressing feelings that may expose what we're truly battling with.

I can't tell you the number of times my wife has asked me questions about certain things that I didn't know the answer to but that she fully expected me to ask my friends. For example, I have a single friend who took some time off from dating to work on himself but he recently started dating again. I've spoken to him many times and all I've asked him is if he believes the woman he's with now is his wife. My wife asked me if my friend was dating and I responded that he was. She wanted to know what her name was. I don't know because I didn't ask. She wanted to know where she was from. I didn't know because I didn't ask. My wife wanted to know what she did for a living. Again, I didn't know because I didn't ask. She was looking for details but I didn't have any to give her.

Nonetheless, feeling weak to a man is the ultimate sign of failure. When you train a boy that his only option is to be strong then he will run from anything that looks weak. Why? Because it goes against his training. His mind is linear. He's trying to follow the rules of the game as they were given because any deviation from those rules means that he has lost the game. And, losing is unacceptable. In fact, weakness to many men is like the feeling right before the final knockout punch.

While watching a boxing match one evening, I sat in front of the television in awe as two boxers fought like champions but there could be only one winner. The challenger threw some really good blows but the champion started coming back towards the end of the fight. He hit an uppercut to the challenger that made him woozy. He fell to the mat for a six count before getting back up on his feet. His legs were wobbly, his hands weren't covering his chin and you could see in his eyes that he was disoriented. He was barely standing up on his own. The champion went in for the knockout punch and connected with a nice right haymaker that floored the challenger to the ground. He was out like a light.

While the knockout punch was special, it wasn't as impactful as when the challenger got back on his feet after being knocked senseless. It was at that point that he was weak. He was vulnerable. He was at his wits end but he stayed in the fight. Why in the world would a man keep fighting even though he's weak? Because that's part of the rules. If you want to quit, then give up! But, if you want to win, you must keep fighting despite your injuries! Those are just the rules of the game. And one thing men are good at doing is playing games. When the game doesn't seem to be in our favor we'll create our own rules to rewrite the game. The challenger was at his weakest but he did not ask for help. He was willing to risk being knocked out rather than looking over and asking for help from everyone in his corner. That's a man's mentality most of the time.

Because many of us avoid the appearance of weakness, we fail to ever reach optimum strength. We don't see our marriage being the best it can be because we refuse to reach out and ask for help. We don't understand how to deal with the pressure of raising our children, especially when we didn't experience it ourselves, so we never reach out and ask for help. We don't see our businesses growing because many of us refuse to ask for help. Instead we'd rather have our marriage end in divorce, our children hate us and our business file bankruptcy before we ever reach out for help. Because asking for help can be seen as a sign of weakness. It is as if we'd rather stagger and trip on our feet while we await the knockout blow. The idea of men gathering to discuss the pressure we feel in our marriage or life is out of the question because talking about it would mean that we're admitting defeat in the ring. We'd rather appear strong on wobbly legs than ask for help on stable ones.

Learning to live with the pressure is a bit different. Notice that I didn't mention that we don't have pressure or that we don't know it exists. The pressure to be strong, the pressure to protect, provide, spend time with the Lord, lead our family spiritually and to accomplish our families purpose on this earth.

Because we are taught to be strong, we normalize these pressures and make it part of how we live. Though we are taught strength, very few of us are ever taught how to deal with the pressure that's brought on from it. Many may not imagine that strong people feel a heavy load of pressure more often than others. We do. This is because usually the weak have to lean on the strong. Have you ever heard of the phrase 'the rock of the family'? This usually refers to the family member that was seen and known as the strength of the family. This is the person people could depend on and openly go to with problems and concerns. She or he was a pillar of courage, stability and honor. To lose that rock would be devastating! Well, being the strong one means you have to be the rock! You are expected to be calm in situations where everyone else is flustered and frustrated. You are expected to be stable in all situations. You are expected to be honorable even when people misuse you. You are expected to be strong all the time, not some of the time. You must have the answers to the problems, the money they need, and the resources they depend on. That is a lot of pressure.

I've oftentimes speculated as to why we hear so much about big momma and grandmother, not grandfather and paw paw. Could it be that the man was expected to be the rock of the family for so long that the weight of pressure crushed him? He saw death as a way to escape the weight of it all. The grave became his way of escape. Trying to be everything for everyone gets tiresome after a while.

Instead of communicating the weight of the pressure to everyone, he remains silent. He keeps going to work, helping everyone with their heavy lifting in his truck, giving money out to those who need it, and being a steady strong voice and hand in the household. He does all of this while the pressure of responsibility crushes his spirit! There's little secret why more men commit suicide than women or why men die years earlier than women—we are stressed by expectations that we refuse to communicate. Instead, we learn to live with them. They become part of our identity and way of living.

This leads to the next reason why men rarely communicate about the pressure we feel from our wives –pressure doesn't really come from our wives or other women, but from ourselves. I should also add that a great deal of the pressure we experience comes from other men inadvertently. We often pressure ourselves into looking, acting, and dressing a certain way because we desire to live up to the pressure that we have placed on ourselves.

We want to make more money so we can buy bigger and better things. We feel the pressure to do it. I know men right now who have multiple jobs because they want their family to live better than how they did growing up. They want to be able to afford to buy their children things they didn't have and give them experiences they didn't receive. I know men who inject steroids into their body to look more muscular because they are self-conscious of how they look. One of the vainest places on this planet is a gym because it allows men to look at other men and compare themselves to how another man looks.

We often hear about women judging themselves by looking at other women but men do it as well. We take steroids, get hair pieces, get plastic surgery, and more to meet the pressures we put on ourselves. We go out and work ourselves into the ground just so we can afford things we really don't need and impress people who couldn't care less. We put these pressures on ourselves to perform and the weight of it all becomes more than we can handle.

My wife was shocked when I told her that most of our pressure doesn't come from our spouse but ourselves. She thought that we felt pressure in marriage from our wives but we cannot give them all the credit. I'm not saying that pressure doesn't exist from our wives and children but I cannot conclude that the majority of how we feel comes from our family.

I am aware of men who feel heavily pressured by their wife to perform and deliver all the time. They feel the pressure of working hard, paying all the bills, communicating all the time, dating her, having good sex regularly (because there's a such thing as bad sex and no man wants to have that), being cordial with her side of the family, spending time with the kids, being the leader of the house and leading them spiritually. That is a heavy task for anyone, and I know many men who have felt the pressure to accomplish everything on the list. The problem is that when we don't feel as if we measure up, we shrink back. Instead of trying to get better, we usually think that it's best to not keep trying. I'll explain it like this.

My mom put me in a basketball camp one summer. I wasn't really aware of my skill level until I started practicing. I was given all the rules so I had a firm grasp of the game. I knew about the basketball, was aware of where to throw it and I knew who to pass it to while playing. My problem wasn't the rules of the game but it was my perceived skill level in comparison to all of the other boys around me. I saw how well they shot in comparison to mine. I saw how they ran, how they dribbled, how they blocked and how they studied the game. I compared it to myself and I was left to conclude that I was not a good basketball player. Instead of trying to get better, I stopped altogether! I figured why should I try to perfect a game that I felt I wasn't skilled in playing.

Instead of trying to work on my skill, I gave it up and moved on to something else. You may find this hard to believe, but men think this way even when it comes to marriage. If they don't feel as if they measure up as a husband, they'd rather leave their marriage than work it out. A lot of men who do stay to work it out only do it because they are afraid of one thing—being alone! It's not that they really want to be married but that they don't want to be alone. He will continue to cheat and lie in the relationship because his heart isn't with his spouse or girlfriend; he still has his heart under lock and key. He's in the relationship because he doesn't want to be alone and even a fool knows that it isn't good to be alone!

The pressure of life weighs us down because we allow them to. We bring them on ourselves and wonder why we feel heavy. One of the main ways we bring on these pressures is through comparison. We look at other men and compare ourselves with them. Men measure everything and whatever doesn't measure up has to go! That's just the way it is. We measure ourselves to each other and the pressure just keeps piling on. We see how much one man can take his family on vacation, so we work harder to afford it for our family as well. We measure whether or not we have more money than our neighbor or if our job title is as great as our brothers. We measure our theology to see who knows more about God. Some men measure their sexual drive and ability by how many partners they sleep with within a given period. We measure our tenacity and drive by how much more we're able to do over the next man beside us. Trust me when I say that we measure everything and it never fails we always come up short somewhere. We bring this added pressure on ourselves.

This last one is a big one! If you are a woman reading this book, you may have felt some kind of way when I said it's tough being a man. You may have said, "How dare he say that it is tough being a man; has he ever tried being a woman?" I want you to understand that the trick of the enemy is to cause the man and the woman to compete against each other. Any good enemy knows that the best way to fight is to destroy from within. His method of choice is comparison. That is why we make statements and arguments that force men and women to compete against each other. Please understand that me making that statement doesn't discount your hardship or struggle; rather, it serves to point out the hardships and pressures felt by men all over this world. We must come to a place as beings where we realize that speaking about one's abilities or difficulties doesn't discount someone else's. It doesn't make us better or worse, it only makes us different. Now, allow me to restate and explain my initial point.

It is tough being a man!

My wife has carried all three of our children. During her pregnancies, she would remind me that she was pregnant and I was not. I will never know the hardship and beauty of childbirth. During one of our talks my wife stressed to me the difficulties of carrying a child. She spoke of her legs aching and cramping, her back hurting, difficulty sitting down for long periods of time, irregularities with sleep and hunger pains. I heard everything she said but there was something I wanted her to understand as well. I told her, "Heather, you are tasked with carrying the child but I am tasked with carrying both of you!" That doesn't minimize her difficulty, it only highlights my responsibility as well. It doesn't make me better; it only shows that we are different in our level of pressure.

As a man, I am expected to be the leader. I am expected to be a place of emotional and financial stability. I'm expected to be strong and wise. When my wife is weak, I am expected to be her knight in shining armor coming to her rescue to save her from whatever or whomever is trying to attack her, even if it's just an unruly call center employee. I'm expected to show up and perform. There are no off-days from being a man. As a husband, my wife leans on me. As a father, my children lean on me. The big problem comes in here—where do I lean when I'm tired? My fellow believers would stress that we must lean on God and they would be accurate. Some would say that we must lean on wise counsel and mentors, and they wouldn't be wrong either. There are even some who would say that we should lean on our wife and I wouldn't fully disagree there. However, I would say that all of the men I have ever discussed this with have made it very clear that they aren't fully open with their wife about everything that burdens them. Why? Because they don't feel that their wife could handle it. They are able to see what their wife can handle by what they pass on to them. By seeing this, they refuse to believe their wife can really handle all of the issues that burdens their heart, so they don't bother telling them everything.

As a pastor, I understand the importance of finding strength in God and leaning on him; however, I understand that even that gets difficult to comprehend at times. There are times when we feel as if God has overlooked us altogether. When we feel as if he isn't there, where do we go? Some would say that we should go to our wise counsel. However, very few men actually have wise counsel nowadays. Many of our elders and fathers are absent and/or silent. This means there are generations of lost boys growing up without guidance, and that's scary! Finally, the men should just confide in their wife, right? Well, what happens when the man doesn't trust his wife? He tells her nothing! I've been around many men who say that they would never tell their wife anything of merit because they know she will tell others. So, where does a man lean when he feels like God is absent, wise counsel is silent and his wife is unfit or too unstable to be trusted with his heart? They do whatever they feel they need to do to drown out the pain. And this world is filled with so many horrible things to lean on.

Many men don't have any direction. Women expect them to get in the driver seat of the car and drive them to success but he doesn't even know how to start it. He doesn't have a roadmap. No one taught him how to change the tire when he runs over unexpected things along their journey. He doesn't know how to put fuel in the car when they're running low on faith. He just doesn't know but he's expected to lead. You might ask, "Well, why doesn't he just ask for help?" Pressure. While my wife and I were driving, I felt as if I missed my turn but I was too prideful to ask for directions. I'd rather go over 20 miles in the wrong direction than simply open my mouth and ask someone to help me along my journey. That's the difficult part of being a man—overcoming the pride of life.

Until we realize the damage that we cause ourselves by taking on and accepting the heavy pressures from others and ourselves, we will continue this dangerous pattern until we are crushed under the weight of it all

***

Whew! That was heavy ladies! As a helpmeet, I want to share my quick perspective on learning to trust my husband to lead. I first stopped nagging him. Of course, the thoughts came into my head "What if we fail? What if things fall apart? What if.." I had to learn that God will hold my husband responsible for what happens within our household and then reward our family for my willingness to support, encourage and pray for my husband (Colossians 3:24). I surrendered to the Lord with this understanding because it was the order that the Lord put into place. After I stopped trying to pressure and control my husband, he started to open up to me. I finally got my husband back! I wasn't trying to control or change him, I only wanted him to be the man that God called him to be.

I have pressures and my husband has pressures. My goal is to not add to his load or compare his pressures to mine. His goal is not to pressure me and to compare his pressures to mine. We search for ways to make life easier for each other. We aren't always perfect but we are a work in progress. We have learned to be empathic to each other's needs and patient with one another's progress. Obviously pressuring him hasn't worked out so far, so let's try something different. Let's win him over with our quiet and gentle spirit. Let's be patient, loving, kind and led by the Holy Spirit when it comes to things we need to bring up in our marriages.

CHAPTER SEVEN
PRESSURE FROM FAMILY AND FRIENDS

The people closest to you have the most impact on who you become, so of course the pressure we feel from them can feel far more intense than outside sources. I truly believe that someone reading this right now is out of position because of someone else's declaration over their life.

Our families can be responsible for planting seeds of anxiety about school, work, having a family, or any number of things. This can lead to a battle in your spirit of not feeling good enough as you are. A battle that you're not living up to their standards or a battle against the fear of failure. Well-meaning family members may have your best interest at heart but their desires for you don't have to be your reality. Maybe your parents want you to be a doctor, lawyer, accountant or to take over the family business but deep down you know that God has called you to something different.

As a parent, I understand what it's like to want the best for your children. But it's better for you to be obedient to the Lord than to what others say, even your parents. If your parents are telling you to do things that God has not convicted you of, then you're in a dangerous place. Deuteronomy 5:16 says, "Honor your mother and Father," but it must be put in proper context. Honoring your parents does not mean making them your god. Your parent's words don't outweigh those words and leading of the Holy Spirit.

As a mother, I ask the Holy Spirit to show me the gifts and talents that he has given Logan, Taylor, and Roman. I want to know what they have been called to do. I want to help them in whatever the Lord has commissioned them for. If that means that Logan doesn't go to college and he takes over the ministry, great. If that means that Taylor goes off to school because she believes the Lord is leading her there, I will support her, help her find scholarships, pay for it and encourage her. If it means that she writes books and takes over Pinky Promise, then that's wonderful. Although I didn't know my degree or what I was doing in college, Jesus met me there in my pit and saved me. I met some of my best friends there and that was my journey.

A friend of mine offered to share his story of family pressure:

I have dealt with pressure in my own life from the ones who loved me enough to give their entire life for me – my parents. They worked hard to achieve success in the face of overwhelming odds and their life's purpose was to have me go further than they ever could.

My parents were raised in the deep south – Louisiana and Tennessee. My mother and father experienced the challenges of growing up in a time of great social conflict but also a time where people of color were beginning to create lives their ancestors only dreamed of. My parents pursued that life with unrelenting bravery. They successfully obtained a higher education and built successful careers in medicine and education, all while obtaining positions of influence and starting a family.

My father was a successful doctor and wanted to pass the family business to me. As a young child this seemed to be a perfect dream. What little boy would not want to follow in the footsteps of his hero? My Dad was the fastest man on a track, the strongest man I knew, and the person who listened to my desires and helped me achieve them. I was sold!

Growing up, I was a young African American male in a southern integrated school, with access to the same opportunities as my white classmates. I also had parents with the heart and resources to guide me along my path. All seemed great until I actually thought to ask myself, "What is my purpose?"

I thought the answer was simple but I began to realize that my purpose seemed to be curated for me without much of my input. I began to see my "purpose" of following in my father's footsteps as a burden to fulfil the dreams of my parents. It wasn't until I was presented with the opportunity to serve others that I started to realize a purpose that I wanted for myself. When I was 16, I was invited on a mission trip that would change my life. On this trip I witnessed God use my gifts to bring hope, light, and service to others.

That experience led me to challenge the narrative already written for me. I felt I was letting my parents down by not fulfilling their dreams for me but I also felt the pressure of knowing it wasn't right in my spirit. As young people we are introduced to many new aspects of our potential: our voices get deeper, we outgrow our jeans, and we begin to see the world from a different perspective; however, we also feel the impact of our raw emotions. During my teenage years, that journey combined with the pressure to follow the path laid before me led to a period of isolation. I isolated myself to find peace. Music was my therapy and laughter was my drug.

Many of my relationships began to feel strained because I could not communicate what I felt but I knew what others saw in me, was not for me. I wanted to pursue full-time ministry as a young adult's pastor but as a part of the interview process for the job, my dad had to agree to my hiring in this role. I was too young to recognize it at the time but my father did not allow me to work in ministry out of protection for me. He made a comment that I will never forget, "If the calling of God is on your life, it will follow you no matter where you go." I felt as if he was not allowing me to build my path and I was shut down.

I went to college still following the path of my parents and I felt happy for them but unfulfilled for me. I was a pre-med student at Louisiana State University and I did well until I met the opposition that separates those who have the passion to be a doctor and those who do not. I met Bio-chemistry 101. It was in failing that class that I realized I did not have the ambition to continue to be a doctor. This was not a phase, I was not undisciplined, I just did not want this for myself.

I left that class and walked to the administration office to change my major. I was a junior so the implications were huge at the time but as I sat with the guidance counselor and we filled out a questionnaire, I found what I was trying to put words to for so long. My questionnaire revealed I should consider a career as a counselor, religious leader, or a job in education. I longed to help people by inspiring hope, working through problems, and coaching through obstacles. I finally had a path towards my purpose.

The pressure that I felt from my parents was lifted as I finally had the tools to build my own future. I remember the conversation like it was yesterday. I told my parents I changed my major and for the first time I could explain what I wanted to do. It was hard for them to hear. I felt bad as if I let them down but I knew that it felt right.

I went on to graduate and start a wonderful career in Human Resources. That career has been filled with many ups and downs; however, my career has never been my purpose. My purpose has been to walk people through discovering the ability that God placed in them. I have seen companies grow and change as we focus on people and not on bottom line dollars. I have spoken at conferences and received recognition for improved employee engagement and improved company culture but a day I will always remember is the day I was ordained as a minister.

My father was there and he was proud of me. At the age of 31, I felt as if I could finally show him that I knew I was right. All my brothers went on to become doctors but I alone was in Human Resources and ministry. As I was ordained, my father conducted the prayer over me. It was during that time he said that I was now the head of the family. I held the highest position as a minister of God's word. It was in that moment that I realized the pressure created the strength to grow."

***

Think about what is on the other side of your obedience. When you stand before God one day, will you say you obeyed God's voice or "the pressures?"

What an amazing story! Thank you Soloman Jordan for sharing.

Friendships

Now, let's talk about your friendships. Do you have any high maintenance friends? Someone who is constantly draining you? You never know what they're thinking, you feel like you are always walking on egg shells, and that person is always mad about something. They call you with their issues and it seems like they always have something going on. They rarely ask you how you're doing and it's very much a one-sided friendship. You almost dread their text messages and phone calls because if you don't respond to one text, they text you with seven more messages while wondering why you haven't responded. You cannot always trust this friend because they aren't consistent or loyal. They gossip about your other friends and constantly pressure you to talk to them. They take advantage but aren't able to give the same as they receive.

This type of friend may not identify with all of the above but if she identifies with a few of the attributes then you may have a high maintenance friend. I have a few people like this in my life and I simply refuse to let them pressure me. I am honest and upfront by letting them know that I have a husband, three kids, a ministry, and several businesses so I won't always have time to be there for them in the ways they would like. I had a lot more friends like this when I was younger and I had to distance myself from many of them because they were too emotional. I was working on not being led by my feelings and it seemed like every time I turned around there was some new drama. I can say that I have created a space in my life where I have a drama free marriage, drama free friends, and a drama free life. I protect mine and my family's peace. I am not telling you to throw these friends away because there is potential for both of you to grow in love and compassion but be led by the Holy Spirit to separate as needed.

If I can be honest, I used to be a high maintenance friend. I would call my best friend the second I had a problem or an issue. When she didn't answer I would blow her phone up. I was so upset! She was supposed to be there for me as a friend. I remember the Holy Spirit telling me that I depended on her way too much and that He wanted me to rely on Him in that way. I cannot imagine the pressure she felt from me. It turns out that my best friend was either very busy or she had left her phone at home. This was only a year after I got saved and my best friend was really the only person I knew who was living for Jesus. I just moved to New York City and I was walking in a very dry season and truly needed a friend but I needed God more. God took me to the wilderness so I could learn to trust in Him like never before and I was using my friend as a crutch. I am thankful for that lesson and I needed to stop depending on her. If you feel convicted by this or you have a friend that may be doing the same things remember that God won't share His glory with anyone else, even if you are a baby in Christ like I was years ago.

Now, I am truly thankful for my low maintenance friends. We don't have to talk every day, our friendship is easy, and we're still friends 18 years later. All of my friends are busy operating in purpose and are pure-hearted, consistent, and trustworthy. I can vent to them and I know it will stay between us and they constantly give me the benefit of the doubt. We can go a month without talking and can pick up like we didn't miss a beat. Our friendship isn't forced and I don't feel pressured to do or be things I'm not. "How can two walk together unless they agree? (Amos 3:3)"

What kind of other friends may you have?

Maybe you have had to leave friends behind who haven't submitted to God in the same way or that may be pressuring you to be who you used to be. Maybe you have taken a stand for God and they have begun to believe negatively about you. What do you do with that pressure? Do you go back to the clubbing, the drugs, the sex, or the sin you used to live in? A friend should push us closer to Jesus, not away from Him.

Friends that don't understand the call on your life or who disagree with it can be used by the enemy to distract you from where God is leading you. When my husband and I went into ministry, we lost a lot of "friends" because they didn't believe in what God called us to do. The pressure to "fit in" and stay comfortable was there but we refused to give into it. We knew that God had called us into ministry and nobody could stop it. You have to be so sure in what God has called you to do that you're willing to be talked about or disagreed with because of it. I can assure you that when you take a stand for God – he will meet you there.

You may begin to experience the pressure of having to separate from many people you once had friendships with. You may even feel pressure to have friends. Instead of letting that pressure get to you, show yourself friendly. Join a bible study group, or a Pinky Promise group in your area (www.pinkypromisemovement.com). Get busy serving in your local church or community. I don't believe God created us to be without friends. No matter how old you are there is no such thing as "no new friends." Don't miss out on a new friendship because of past hurts. Press forward. Be an amazing friend and trust your discernment as you are led by the Holy Spirit.

CHAPTER EIGHT

PRESSURE IN MINISTRY

I am a first-generation preacher. I was totally "green" when we started our ministry but I was so excited! I wanted to tell everyone about it. I would pass out flyers in grocery stores and I was truly passionate about everyone living for Jesus. But we had no clue what it meant to plant a church – the financial responsibility, insurance, forming ministries within the church and a million other details were all new to us. We were literally clueless.

Years later I am still excited about people coming to church and I still invite them but I have been able to gain perspective. When we first got started, I felt pressure to make sure we were on TV and radio, that we had expensive equipment, and that everything was perfectly in line for the people who would visit with us. I was caught up in the details. Our very first service, we planned for at least 200 guests but only four people showed up.

We felt alot of pressure to keep going even when things continued to stand in our way weekly. There was a time when the school's custodian didn't show up to unlock the doors and we had to have church outside. We rented other locations like hotels and college classrooms but deep down, I knew it wasn't time for our church. I wanted so bad for it to be time. We announced it to family friends and the few people that followed us on social media, so quitting would make us look like failures. I felt pressure from every side but deep down I knew that God had told us to shut it down. I recall the day we decided to put the ministry aside for a season − I was driving by a stadium and the Lord told me that one day, we would be preaching in stadiums.

Stadiums, Jesus? Not only did you tell me to shut down our church where there were only four people every Sunday but you're telling me that we are going to preach in stadiums? Okay, I want to believe you but help me with my unbelief. We needed to move from Atlanta to Mississippi for a season but once we returned, I felt like we were back where we were supposed to be and that we were home for good. By then, we were busy building Pinky Promise and the Lord laid it on our hearts to establish our church, The Gathering Oasis, again. This time in Atlanta. This time in God's timing. I have learned that when you first start ministry in any capacity, from serving to leading you go through a test of character. Will you be faithful to the call even if people don't show up? Even if only one person comes? Does that one person's soul matter to you? Or do you feel so much pressure and pride to have such a "successful" church that one person isn't enough – you want thousands. Thousands are great but before we saw thousands at our conferences, we started with four. God taught my husband and I to be faithful with four and to preach like there's 4,000 people there. Our pride and ego says that we aren't successful if we aren't on a stage with great numbers but Jesus wants to know if you're willing to leave the 99 in the field to go search for the "one."

I want the one. I care about their soul. You aren't just some person reading my book. You're a SPIRIT that lives in a body. I want to see you in heaven. I want to hug you and say, "Girl, we made it!!!" It was ALL WORTH IT! We get to be with Jesus forever! I want to see you living radically for Christ, loving him, loving others, and walking by faith in your calling. You aren't just $14.99 to me and you definitely aren't just one person to God. The very number of hairs on your head have been counted and placed with intention. As I write my books I pray for the people that read them because I don't know what you need but the Holy Spirit knows how to meet you where you are. He's so good to us.

Back to ministry, I recall when I was serving at my old church and I felt overlooked. I would give ideas and nobody would seem to care. Then, I would get to a conference and they would USE all of my ideas. I wanted so bad to get the credit. I had to check myself on the motives of my heart. Why did I want the credit so bad? I took that to the Holy Spirit and I realized that it was my pride and ego that created a pressure in me to feel "seen." Was it not enough that the Holy Spirit saw me give those ideas? Was it not enough that God gave me those ideas? I contributed nothing, they were His ideas all along.

As a generation, we want to be seen and acknowledged so bad. Why do we want the credit? If we aren't getting our way or "advancing" in our own life, we want to quit the ministry part and find another ministry that will give us our recognition.

Ephesians 6:7 tells us "to work enthusiastically as unto God, not people." Are you serving enthusiastically as unto the Lord or as unto the pat on the back you want someone to give you? I wanted people to see my gifts and talents and tell me that I was talented.

I soon realized that if God sees me, that's more than enough. Thank you Jesus that my reward is in heaven. I served privately for years before I started preaching full time and writing books. Years. Years of being ignored. Years of people talking about me and of being overlooked by my peers. I was saved for 9 years before I saw fruit of what God called me to do. And even then, I didn't need a stage. I was so satisfied with Jesus alone. He was all I needed. He still is all I need.

Stages are great, but I really like kneeling before the Father in my prayer time. I love laying down and sensing the Holy Spirit hug and comfort me. I love journaling my heart out to Jesus and asking the Holy

Spirit how He's doing today. I love our alone time. You see, your private victories birth public victories. It may take years and you may not even see it on this earth because Jesus can return at any moment, but who cares? I can no longer be pressured by people when it comes to ministry.

My heart is not in their words or thoughts because how they feel about me can change at any point. I am thankful for the growth of our church but I recognize that these are God's ministries. We are simply managers of what He has given us. If I am doing everything that I do for the glory of the Father, then my eyes cannot be on what I can see or who is trying to pressure me. I love Acts 2:47 "And THEN God added to their numbers." This tells me there is a process before we are trusted with more.

This way of thinking is hard for us to accept – that we don't have control over the growth of the ministries we have been trusted with. If you take credit for the growth of your ministry, you will also take credit when people leave. You will make it all about you and it's not about you, it's about Jesus and him accomplishing his work on this earth.

Let's think about Satan when he was in heaven, leading worship:

> "How you are fallen from heaven, O shining star, son of the morning! You have been thrown down to the earth, you who destroyed the nations of the world. For you said to yourself, 'I will ascend to heaven and set my throne above God's stars. I will preside on the mountain of the gods far away in the north. I will climb to the highest heavens and be like the Most High.' Instead, you will be brought down to the place of the dead, down to its lowest depths. (Isaiah 14:12-15)"

"For you said to yourself, I, I, I." It was all about "I" and if ministry is ALL about "I" then it no longer becomes effective. Satan got kicked out of heaven because he wanted to BE God. We and he could never be God. Wanting to be acknowledged for your effort is wanting to have the glory for yourself instead of for God. We go to the world to listen to their advice and become hard-hearted towards what God is telling us to do. My prayer is that no matter how our ministry grows, that I will remain humble and softened to the leading of the Holy Spirit. I never want to get caught up in the spirit of "I." I never want to honor someone because their name is "big" and ignore the nameless. Both are important to God. Both are important to me.

If you're feeling pressure in ministry take your eyes off of yourself and put your eyes on Christ. Your "one" is just as important as "one thousand." Success is obedience to God's word. Success is you staying in your lane and saying "yes," to God when all of hell is breaking loose or when your bank account isn't lining up. We could barely pay our bills and those of the church during our first years but when God commissions you to do something on this earth, you get the honor of doing that thing – gladly.

There may also come a time when you will experience pressure from the members of your church. This isn't the time to bend into everybody else's needs or to try and please everyone. People will test you and question your credibility, especially as you're first starting out but you must know the vision that the Lord has given you. We live in a "what's next" generation that wants you to constantly go big or go home, but don't give into that. Run your race well and with godly intention.

I always tell people to have thick skin and a tender heart. I refuse to let people change who I am. Ministry requires that you are in a constant vulnerable state; where you are doing life with people and being transparent with them about your own daily struggle. Yes, this exposes us to the opportunity of betrayal but look at Jesus and his disciples. Jesus knew long before it actually happened that Judas would be the one to betray him. Would you still serve, wash Judas' feet, and love him knowing that he was going to be the one that betrayed you? Every opportunity of discord, though it may be painful to our flesh, is an opportunity for unconditional love.

Let's look at 1 Corinthians 13:1-3:

> "If I speak in the tongues of men or of angels, but do not have love, I am only a resounding gong or a clanging cymbal. If I have the gift of prophecy and can fathom all mysteries and all knowledge, and if I have a faith that can move mountains, but do not have love, I am nothing. If I give all I possess to the poor and give over my body to hardship that I may boast, but do not have love, I gain nothing."

"If I have the faith to move mountains but I don't have love, I am nothing." What is love?

> Love is patient, love is kind. It does not envy, it does not boast, it is not proud. It does not dishonor others, it is not self-seeking, it is not easily angered, it keeps no record of wrongs. Love does not delight in evil but rejoices with the truth. It always protects, always trusts, always

hopes, always perseveres. 1 Corinthians 13:4-7

The Lord's definition of love is the exact opposite of the world's idea of love. This world's idea is, "I love you only when you love me." It says, "Remember who hurt you, pay them back, get angry, remind people of what they did." But how will you develop in godly love unless you get tested with "unlovely people?"

Some of you have left ministries and churches when all God was trying to do is develop you in *his* love. He just wanted you to pass the test of overcoming evil with good, forgiving people and keeping it moving, but you keep running every time you get hurt. God will not trust us with more if it is evident that we have not matured in the love he calls us to. You will encounter people that are worse than those you ran from when you get to your next destination.

When I was a child, I talked like a child, I

thought like a child, I reasoned like a child. When I became a man, I put the ways of childhood behind me. For now, we see only a reflection as in a mirror; then we shall see face to face. Now I know in part; then I shall know fully, even as I am fully known. 1 Corinthians 13:10

Use the pressures that come your way in ministry to develop in love, patience, and hope. Only God can change the heart of man but you can use the hurt those people may cause to further mature yourself in the ways of Christ.

CHAPTER NINE

RUN YOUR OWN RACE

You will constantly feel like you're trying to catch up when you compare yourself to others. I want you to realize that you are purposed and you don't have to copy anybody else's visions or ideas. You don't have to compare their season to your season. You don't have to pursue get rich schemes, chase money or kiss up to anyone in order to see the vision that God has called you to. You simply have to stay in your lane and in obedience to the father.
– The Purpose Room by Heather Lindsey

What are you facing right now? Are you afraid to walk in your lane because nobody else has done it, or are you frustrated because the "market is oversaturated," or because someone took an idea of yours? We are all uniquely created in the way we see and experience things. There is no new idea under the sun but we are different in how we experience and approach fulfilling those ideas. The fear of being like someone else or doing something that someone has already succeeded at is a tool the enemy uses to keep us from fulfilling our talents and gifts.

Imagine if Target never opened because there were too many big box value stores? Or, if Delta Airlines bowed out after filing for bankruptcy in 2005? I can go on and on about huge companies that started from nothing or that simply kept going after facing adversity. Whatever God has for you is for you and it doesn't matter what statistics exist that state otherwise. God will truly open doors for you that no man will close.

Hear me out, God will fund whatever He is telling you to do, you simply have to take the steps of faith as you are instructed. There should be pressure where we are obedient to the Lord. That good pressure moves us to a sense of urgency to be obedient. We must not sit around and act like God hasn't called us all to something. For some, he has called you to start your own business, to others, he has called you to work in corporate America, to some, he has called you to work from home or be a stay at home mom. Whatever God has called you to be, OWN your lane and walk boldly in it. God is gracing you to be in your lane, he doesn't grace and fund us to be in somebody else's lane.

There was a time when I got out of my lane. I was dating a guy and I told him that God called me to preach. He really didn't believe me. He told me that I needed to go back to school and pursue more education to get a more stable job. I literally felt like I wasn't good enough for him with just my 4-year degree. If I could talk to my younger self, I definitely would have shown him the quickest way out of my life because I *knew* God didn't call me back to school.

Going back to grad school wasn't in the plan but I went back to feel valued, to feel worth. It cost me so much. Not only my time, but my energy, money and opportunities to be close to God while I was pursuing something outside of his will for me. I let the voice of a man push me to make a $20,000 mistake and I lost my most valuable asset, my TIME. But it was never his fault because I knew better and so do you. At that time, I didn't know that my value, identity and worth was in Jesus.

If you are doing something and you are in blatant disobedience, then you need to put that thing down and walk away. Are you spending time, energy, and money going into somebody else's lane? Your gift will make room for you. I had a desire to help women and I thought that there was a certain path that I had to take in order to get there but God reminded me:

> Trust in the LORD with all your heart; do not depend on your own understanding. In part of your ways, acknowledge him and he will direct your paths. Proverbs 3:5-6

We may know we are called to a certain thing and in our eagerness to get there, jump ahead of the process or the steps God is directing. We create our own path to success instead of following the lane etched out for us. We must acknowledge Him in all things so that we don't end up in situations we were never called to be in — all in the name of heading towards our "calling."

The scripture says to acknowledge God in ALL of our ways. Everything is included. If I would have acknowledged the Lord he would have not only told me to break things off with that man, but that I did not need another degree at that time.

When I first met that ex, the Lord told me right away, "No, that's not it."

I kept saying, "BUT LORD! I am going to do things right! I am going to do things your way!"

God still doesn't approve of plans that you come up with just because you tag his name to it. Referencing scripture in the midst of mess doesn't make it right. The destination you're heading to will only get worse if you remain in disobedience.

Maybe some of you are like me, pursuing a degree, a career or a relationship that you know is not blessed by God. Instead of taking a step of faith and saying yes to the Lord, you are remaining in sin all while looking for God's approval.

I am reminded of Jonah's story:

In Jonah 1:1-3, Jonah ran from the Lord.

> The word of the Lord came to Jonah son of Amittai: "Go to the great city of Nineveh and preach against it, because its wickedness has come up before me."
> But Jonah ran away from the Lord and headed for Tarshish. He went down to Joppa, where he found a ship bound for that port. After paying the fare, he went aboard and sailed for Tarshish to flee from the Lord.

Nineveh was an ancient Assyrian city on the east bank of the Tigris River of what is now Northern Iraq. Jonah ran because Iraq was worse than it is now.

The people there hated God. Put yourself in Jonah's shoes for a moment. Jonah's "lane" was for him to go to Nineveh and to preach against the wickedness that was there. He saw how wicked the people were, was intimidated, and didn't feel qualified to be their leader. Would you? What if God sent you to a place like Iraq or somewhere else where you weren't totally comfortable?

God may send us to places where things are hard. We will suffer, people will talk about us, throw us under the bus and hate us without a cause. We will go through tests and trials but we will also have breakthroughs and God will be with us along the journey.

Jonah was looking for a way out of the lane God had already told him was his. So, instead of heading in the right direction towards Nineveh, Jonah ran away from the Lord and headed towards Tarshish. Running from God is always a good indicator that you're heading in the wrong direction. Running from

God is also a sure sign that you are headed for judgment and destruction.

> Then the Lord sent a great wind on the sea, and such a violent storm arose that the ship threatened to break up. All the sailors were afraid and each cried out to his own god as they threw the cargo into the sea to lighten the ship.
>
> But Jonah had gone below deck, where he lay down and fell into a deep sleep. The captain went to him and said, "How can you sleep? Get up and call on your god! Maybe he will take notice of us so that we will not perish."
>
> Then the sailors said to each other, "Come, let us cast lots to find out who is responsible for this calamity." They cast lots and the lot fell on Jonah. So they asked him, "Tell us, who is responsible for making all this trouble for us? What kind of work do you do? Where do you come from? What is your country? From what people are you?" "I am a Hebrew and I worship the Lord, the God of heaven, who made the sea and the dry land." Jonah 1:4-9

The other sailors began freaking out. They yelled at him, "WHAT HAVE YOU DONE?" You know it's something when even unbelievers can see your disobedience. Nonetheless, it was Jonah's idea to be thrown off of the boat but the men didn't want Jonah to perish. Running from God not only brought Jonah to a troubled place but he exposed others to the consequences of his disobedience. Other lives were on the line due to his inability to stay true to the lane God had set before him.

Your disobedience is costly. It will cost the people around you their time, energy, and money. Not only did Jonah's disobedience almost cost the lives of those on the boat, but those on the boat lost money because they threw cargo off the boat in the efforts to save lives. You not staying in your own lane will affect those close to you because we are not given a purpose for our own salvation but so that others will see God in our willingness to follow him.

Later, God sends a whale to swallow Jonah and he is in the whale for three days and three nights. The whale spits him up onto the shore and he lives, is repentant, and heads back in the direction of which God has called him – Nineveh.

I wonder how many of you would have stayed on that boat and pressed your way into Tarshish knowing they weren't supposed to be there? How many signs does God have to show you that you're not headed in the right direction? How many times does he have to close doors? How many times does he have to strip you from everything to the point where you only trust in Him alone?

Some of you guys "endured" the boat, went to Tarshish and rented out an apartment. You got a job and you began to create an entire life in a place where God never sent you. Then, you felt like you were in too deep and you didn't want to be embarrassed, so instead of saying yes to God and being obedient to Him – you continued to build a life far away from the place where God sent you. And, for some reason – we think that God is supposed to bless us when we are out of position. If I would have stayed in grad school, I would have been out of position.

I cringe at the thought of what would have happened if I stayed on the path of grad school when I knew that God had different plans for me.

This is also why we must stop looking at other people's lives and wonder why our "blessings" don't look like their blessings. Some people have created entire lives in Tarshish and we are envying disobedience and we don't even know it. We are jealous of somebody else's life but they are out of position.

Once Jonah made it to Nineveh, he preached and EVERYONE got saved:

> Jonah began by going a day's journey into the city, proclaiming, "Forty more days and Nineveh will be overthrown." The Ninevites believed God, a fast was

proclaimed, and all of them, from the greatest to the least, put on sackcloth. Jonah 3:4-5)

Once Jonah realized his mistake in running from God, he returned to his lane and bore fruit. People were saved and believed God because Jonah accepted his calling. This is a great example that it is never too late to repent for your disobedience and still be useful in God's plans for you. If you've been going in the wrong direction for a while, you can turn around and say "yes" at any time and he will use you as he always intended. God is always waiting for you to return to Him.

I challenge you to run your own race. You may be thinking that you don't know where that is just yet but you can practice hearing the voice of God so that when he speaks you will not miss your instructions. Spend time with him daily and meditate on his promises over your life. There is no way that anyone knows more about you than the one who created you but we must do the work to realize who we are in him. We simply have to be willing and expectant of the chance to hear God's voice.

Remember that God doesn't bless the lane you create. He blesses His plans for your life. Trust Him. He has your back.

CHAPTER TEN

GODLY PRESSURE VS WORLDLY PRESSURE

Is it really possible to be free from the pressures of this world? The Bible says because we're in the world, we will have tribulation, or pressure. But we must understand that there is a difference between godly pressure and worldly pressures.

In the beginning, God's plan was that we be free from pressure. The garden of Eden was a place of perfect peace. God didn't put any pressure on Adam and Eve; all they had to do was obey Him. Easy enough right? Pressure came through Satan in the form of temptation and doubt. Satan is still putting pressure on people to this day. When Adam and Eve fell, Satan became the god of this world. And now by simply being in the world, we will experience tribulation. Their failure to obey opened the door to a fallen world, one where we must always be prepared for the battles the enemy will use to keep us distracted from our closeness with God.

> For we wrestle not against flesh and blood, but against principalities, against powers, against the rulers of the darkness of this world, against spiritual wickedness in high places. Ephesians 6:12

Though we may not see it, we are all in a wrestling match in this world. We're struggling against something in the spiritual realm. This fight is not a flesh and blood fight. To win, we have to recognize that Satan is Roaring around like a lion, looking for someone to destroy (1 Peter 5:8).

If we neglect to understand that there is a real battle on this earth, then we will be completely surprised when we are being tested and tried. Although we already know that the fight is WON through Jesus Christ, we still have work to do on this earth before we meet Jesus face to face. Satan's goal is to keep us distracted through the battle to keep us from serving God. We can't fight with a clear mind if we're consumed with our emotions and internal pressures.

Don't allow the enemy to use this tactic against you.

How does he pressure us? He sends people and thoughts into our hearts that say things like this:

- "You aren't enough. If you only did "this" you would have some value"

- "You will never be enough. You're going to end up like so and so."

- "You aren't pretty enough, you need to wear your hair like this and wear makeup to cover your flaws."

- "You aren't smart. Remember what that teacher told you when you were growing up? She was right. You will never amount to anything unless you get multiple degrees to prove them wrong"

- "You are still single at 30? What is wrong with you? You should hurry up and find a man. Your clock is ticking."

- "Your child doesn't know the Chinese alphabet at three like my kid? Wow, maybe you should spend your life savings to put him in a better school."

- "You're not doing as much as other entrepreneurs online. You should do more. Post more about your business."

- "Wow, that's it? Only 5 people showed up to your book club? I had 100 people show up to mine."

- "You know, you should preach and run your ministry more like those ministers on Instagram."

- "So, when you are guys going to have kids after you get married?"

- "So and so just got to the church and they already have a leadership position. When are you getting one? Are they overlooking you?"

Do you see where I'm going with this? All of this pressure can DROWN you out and make you feel like you will never, ever have it all together. Satan will send well-meaning people to do his work by planting seeds of doubt.

In every interview I get asked, "Heather, what's next?"

My old thinking: I need to give them an answer that makes them think that I'm progressively moving forward. It needs to be more exciting than what I am currently doing."

My current thinking: "I don't know. I don't have a 5, 10, or 20-year plan. My plan is to wake up every morning and spend time with Jesus and take the life I have one day at a time." Yes, I have Pinky Promise Conferences planned every year. I'm writing a new book, running a ministry with my husband and trying to balance it all. God typically opens up the doors along the way and He shows me the way. I didn't think I would have a TV show and I did. I didn't seek after it. I didn't think I would get invited to be on reality TV shows on a regular basis, but it happens. I don't walk through 100% of those doors because the shows don't line up with my beliefs but I have learned that if I seek the Lord, He will truly add whatever I need onto me.

When that family member comes skipping along to ask you about your single status, remind them that God's timing is perfect and you trust Him. Your clock isn't ticking. Sarah was pregnant at 99 years old. When that person wonders why your ministry is so "small" remind them that God also cares about the "one" and that you must be faithful with small in order to be trusted with more.

When people try to question you about leaving college, ask them if they're going to pay your student loans or if they were with God when he wrote his plans for your life. I think one of the most powerful things you can say is "I don't know." Who said that we had to have everything figured out? Even the person asking you the question doesn't have life completely figured out.

I recall a time in my life where God specifically told me not to work for a season. It was only two months, but you can imagine that it was a long couple of months. My boyfriend at the time told me "that there is no way that God told me not to work during that time." Now, I was going through a season where my worth an identity was in money and my job title. I truly needed to be stripped from all of these things so I could have a proper perspective. My contract also ended with one job and for an entire month I was applying for jobs and nothing was opening up. I was just a single girl and I was ok with not working. Nobody was depending on me for anything. I was so frustrated for that month of applying. I couldn't even get referral jobs. I knew the scriptures about being lazy and "if a man doesn't work, you don't eat." I wasn't lazy. I was applying, I was asking around. I ran to the feet of the Lord one day and I was so frustrated. I asked the Lord why I couldn't get a job? He told me to "rest" and to not put my energy into applying because it would take a little bit of time before that door would open again."

It was assuring to me because I knew I could labor in the flesh or I could labor in faith. If I stepped out in my own ability, I would be outside of where God wanted me during that time. I definitely felt the pressure to pay my bills and rent but I knew what God told me. And, He totally provided for me during those two months. He began to give me wisdom on what to do and I still had a place to stay and food to eat.

There are clear indicators of godly pressure:

- It always lines up biblically
- You will have peace
- It will confirm what you believe God wanted you to do
- He will confirm it in prayer
- You will feel conviction

The more time I spend with Jesus, the more I can

differentiate whether the pressure I feel is worldly or of the Lord. John 10:27 says, "My sheep listen to my voice; I know them, and they follow me. "After he has gathered his own flock, Jesus walks ahead of them, and they follow him because they know his voice. They won't follow a stranger; they will run from him because they don't know his voice. (John 10:4-5)" The voice of the Holy Spirit does not bring shame or doubt. It is gentle, encouraging but also firm. You will quickly be able to differentiate godly vs. worldly pressured based on what you continuously feed your mind. You cannot possibly watch trash television, listen to secular music, go to the club, drink and smoke, and have sex whenever while still being led by the Spirit. In order to hear from and be led by the Lord, you have to be surrendered to him in all areas of your life. It's simply saying, "God, you call the shots in my life, not me."

If you're struggling with surrendering to God right now, I challenge you to put this book down and surrender right now by faith. I know you are still trying to figure out what that looks like but instead of trying to calculate God, just obey Him. Take it one day at a time.

We want the leading and guiding of the Holy Spirit but we don't want to listen to Him in the process. When God is molding us into his image, we may feel pressured by the Holy Spirit on the inside us to leave a job, leave a relationship, or to move to a certain place. **This is good pressure.** Thank God for the pressure and the tugging of the Holy Spirit!

What I am assured of on this earth is that even Jesus was pressured to the point where he sweat BLOOD.

> Being in agony, Jesus prayed very fervently; and His sweat became like drops of blood, falling down to the ground. Luke 22:44

Jesus knew that he was about to drink the cup of wrath and take on the sins of ALL of humanity. What a heavy load. He was praying and felt the pressure of the world's sin. Although that's a pressure that none of us ever have to feel, and I'm sure it didn't feel good, it was still in the will of God for his life. We all have to go through godly pressure to become who God has called us to be. I have been yelled at, threatened, ignored, rejected, and abandoned but I am thankful because it has made me who I am today. Now that I know who I am in Christ Jesus, I guard my heart against worldly pressure that breeds anxiety, fear, and doubt in my heart. I take pressure from the Lord because he wants what is best for me.

Pressure from God will sometimes be uncomfortable but it bears fruit and leads to freedom from the worldly pressures. God allows difficult situations to come our way so that we may mature from spiritual milk to solid food – the things we need to sustain us on the journey he has for us.

CHAPTER ELEVEN

FREEDOM FROM PRESSURE

Thus far we have identified our identity in Christ and what that means as we battle the daily pressures of this world.

I truly believe that with the power of the Holy Spirit, we can overcome any pressure the enemy brings upon us. God has given us the victory over everything, even death through Jesus Christ! Remember that pressures come at everyone ALL day long. It's up to us to sign for the package of pressure. What we put within us will come out of us when those tests come our way. *What you store up in your quiet time with the Lord will cover you in the midst of the storm.*

Our reactions to the pressures of life are defined by what we feed ourselves daily. Our response to pressure reveals our maturity. Do you break under pressure when you get around family every Thanksgiving? At some point, you have to grow from that – face it and respond in a godly way.

Do you break when you see a really pretty girl online and you start to compare your size to hers? You see, it's easy for you to be confident and bold at church on Sunday or at the Pinky Promise Conference. You're surrounded and victorious on Sunday morning. You're praising God, serving in church and you're with those who do life with you. But what about when you go home and face those pressures? What about when you go to that job that you don't love so much? You can say that you're free but if you get there and allow for someone else's promotion to make you feel less about where you are in life, it's a sure sign that you can be easily provoked.

Pressures and tests show what areas we need to be freed from in order to grow.

No matter how much I have "matured" or "grown" in my walk with Jesus – I realize that I have a continual need for God to do a deep work in my heart.

We justify the way we feel as "righteous" but if we ask the Lord to correct our hearts, He would tell us to grace others the way that He graces us. We will never have it all together but thank God for Jesus. His strength is best perfected in weakness. We cannot measure our chapter three to somebody else's chapter twelve– there is truly a season under the sun for every part of our life so we must learn to be content whether we are reaping or planting.

Through the power of the Holy Spirit, we all can be victorious in our everyday lives. We can overcome the devil and our flesh. We can be ministers of peace and reconciliation on this earth and walk in perfect communion with God. We can be free from pressure by learning to yield to the Lord and resisting the devil (James 4:7). The Bible says that the devil will flee with his pressure. How do we resist the devil? By speaking the word of the Lord over our situation. If we are being pressured with fearful thoughts, we should quote scriptures that speak of victory over fear.

> For God hath not given us the spirit of fear, but of power, and of love, and a sound mind. 2 Timothy 1:7

> Yea, though I walk through the valley of the shadow of death, I will fear no evil: for thou art with me; thy rod and thy staff they comfort me. Psalm 23:4

> The Lord is my light and my salvation; whom shall I fear? The Lord is the strength of my life; of whom shall I be afraid? Psalm 27:1

> In righteousness shalt thou be established: thou shalt be far from oppression; for thou shalt not fear: and from terror; for it shall not come near thee. Isaiah 54:14

As Christians, we have victory over pressure and tribulation because of God's promises to us. Praise the Lord! Our Savior died for nothing less than that. In order for you to walk boldly in what God has called you to do, you have to be willing to break free from the pressure that has kept you distracted and off track.

In order for you to walk boldly in what God has called you to do, you have to be free from the pressure. Is it really possible in this world to be free from the pressures of it? I think that another fancy word for freedom from pressure is freedom from people bondage.

You can't care what people think of you.

Are you listening to me? You simply cannot care.

People are going to think a certain way about you and measure you based on what is considered "success" in their eyes. For example, someone may look at my life and say that I am not successful because I do not work for corporate America or I'm not a "doctor" or a "nurse" a "lawyer" or an "accountant." I'm a preacher and an entrepreneur. I own several of my own small businesses that I created as I was led by the Holy Spirit.

So, someone may judge my life and think, well, "maybe you should go back to school, get your doctorate and become a clinical psychologist."

My response:

That is not what God has called me to be.

He has called me first to my family and then to share Jesus with a broken and hurting world to bring peace and comfort to people through the sharing of preaching. I don't have the time and energy to get onto a field that I know God hasn't called me to walk in. And right now, some of you are walking in a certain area or you're headed to school for a certain thing because you feel pressured by people to be something other than what God has called you to be.

We do not select a career or purpose based on

money or even legacy. We must recognize that our identity is in Jesus Christ and what He did for us on the Cross. He gave us value. He gave us worth. He gave us identity. Not a piece of paper. Not some degree. Not your family being proud of you because you obeyed them and disobeyed God. Not your "clock ticking." I'm gonna tell you this really quick about marriage – if your identity is in a wedding ring on your finger, then you will put a bunch of pressure on your husband to have the perfect marriage. You will even settle because you think that God is taking too long. You don't love yourself so instead of waiting on God's timing, you marry whosever is willing. Remember that marriage doesn't solve loneliness, it just changes the physical act of being alone. You can still have a whole husband in the bed with you and feel lonely. I truly believe that pressure is a distraction from the enemy to get you focused on what you do not have in your life right now. Remember that an event in life is not the answer to your problems. Surrendering to Jesus and letting Him take all of who you are is an *answer* to your problems.

In discussing freedom from pressure, I want you to understand that as mentioned in the previous chapter, there is good pressure. This pressure comes on from life to develop you into who God called you to be. There IS good pressure. It's vital that you recognize that you don't want to be free from GOOD pressure. Let's look at some more "good pressure" in the bible.

The Potter and the Clay – Isaiah 64:8 tells us, "And Yet, O Lord, you are our Father. We are the clay and you are the potter. We are all formed by your hand."

If you think about the way clay is made, water and pressure is applied to mold and create the clay.

Now, let's look at Job. Job lost everything and felt pressured by his friends to deny God. Even in the midst of losing his family and cattle he proclaimed, "Though He slay me, I will hope in him. I will surely defend my ways to His face. (Job 13:15)" Other versions of the bible say, "Even IF he kills me, yet I will trust in him." It's safe to say that Job felt PRESSURE. But, in the midst of the world's pressure, Job clung to the Lord and said, "Even if he wipes me out, I will trust in him alone."

Even though you're being pressured on every side continue to trust in the Lord. Don't deny God in those hard moments. Cling to Him. Job had freedom because he knew that his fate was not in this world. But eternally with Jesus.

I think of Jesus being tempted by Satan in Matthew 4:1—Jesus was fasting for 40 days and 40 nights. God allowed his very best to be tempted by Satan only for him to demonstrate his power through scripture to shut him down. After Jesus uses his authority through scripture, Satan flees from Jesus – we have that same power as well! You don't have to accept that negative, ungodly, worldly pressure!

Now, there are times where you will go through

pressure and tests. For example, when I was single, I was feeling pressured to be SINGLE. I knew that the Holy Spirit was LEADING me gently to be single. Someone may not call it pressure but I knew that I needed to be single for a season because I kept a boyfriend and made him my idol. When I got married, I felt convicted or pressured to respect my husband when I wanted to pop off at the mouth at him. My flesh was screaming to "tell him off" but I felt like I needed to do the right thing. At times, when God is molding us into His image, we may feel pressured by the Holy Spirit on the of inside us to leave a job, leave a relationship, move to a certain place or whatever else. This is good pressure. Thank God for the "pressure" and the "tugging's" of the Holy Spirit! I recall a time where I had a shopping problem in college. Whenever I had a rough day, I went to the outlet malls near our school. I remember shopping in Forever 21 and I only can tell you all with urgency like the Lord told me – He told me to "GET

OUT!!" I dropped my clothes and ran out of that store. I looked back and thought, "Is the store about to crumble?? Is there going to be a shooting?? Why would the Lord challenge me like that??" The Lord showed me, "No, there will be no disasters. The issue wasn't the store, but your motive and your heart. You use shopping as a void filler."

Welp.

I sure felt pressure that day. But, it was good pressure. Pressure to do the RIGHT thing and I was being pressured by the RIGHT ONE, the Holy Spirit.

What I am assured of on this earth is that even Jesus was pressured to the point where He sweat BLOOD. In Luke 22:44 "Being in agony, Jesus prayed very fervently; and His sweat became like drops of blood, falling down to the ground." Here, Jesus knew that He was about to drink the cup of wrath and take on the sins for ALL of humanity. What a HEAVY load. The pressure he felt was during His prayer time. He was praying and He felt the pressure from the sin of this world. Although that's a pressure that none of us ever have to feel, I'm sure that pressure didn't feel good. And, it was still in the will of God for His life.

I have had to go through GOOD PRESSURE to become who God has called me to be. I have been yelled at, threatened, ignored, rejected, abandoned and whatever else and I am thankful for the pressure because it's made me who I am today. Now that I know who I am in Christ Jesus, I guard my heart against BAD pressure. I take pressure from the Lord because clearly, He wants me to grow or change in some areas. I know that I am not perfect. I desperately need the Lord to change me into His image. The beautiful thing about the Holy Spirit is that He will show you how to discern what is good pressure and what is bad pressure. You will never be completely "free" from pressure on this earth until we face Jesus but we can learn what is godly pressure and what is worldly pressure. I declare that from this point forward, you guard your heart against bad pressure and you only welcome good, godly pressure. My prayer is that you use the pressure to mold you into the vessel that God called you to be.

My prayer is that you will be bold, courageous and willing to follow Jesus no matter what. My prayer is that no matter how hard it gets, you continue to trust in Him. I pray that you reject this world's pressure and hold tight to who God called you to be. If you look at the origin of a diamond, it's interesting to me that a volcano has to happen in order for a diamond to be birthed. At times, you may have to go through some developing in order to get to where God has called you to be. I have had my share of "volcanos" – but I've come out like a pure diamond, strong with clarity on what God has called me to do and WHO He has called me to be. This world can try to tempt me, pressure me, tell me that I need to be something else in order to have worth, but it's much too late. I know WHO I am and WHOSE I am in Jesus Christ.

And, so do you.

I pray that this book ministered to you! I pray that you always stay focused on what God has called you to do and you never stray from his leading.

You can check out my other books on www.pinkypromiseboutiques.com or Amazon, Kindle, Audible Books, IBooks:

1. *Pink Lips & Empty Hearts:* For the Woman who is totally fabulous on the outside but inside is broken, torn apart and feeling empty. This book will fill you up and remind you of your true identity in Jesus.

2. *A Perfect Recipe:* This is for anyone who wants to start eating better plus have more discipline in their food + exercise. It's a devotional and recipe book.

3. *The Runaway Bride*: This is for anyone who has been running from the Lord in any area. We must recognize that we are first the bride of Christ and if our relationship with Him isn't right then no other relationship will work.

4. *Dusty Crowns: Dusting yourself off and breaking free from the distractions to be who God called you to be.* This book will highlight anything that is distracting you from becoming who God called you to be. I challenge you to make sure that your external is as fabulous as your internal. We aren't "dusty" crowns. We are royal crowns and it starts with our heart.

5. *The Purpose Room*: This book is for anyone who is struggling with their purpose and who God called them to be. If you need direction on what God called you to do, this is it!

6. *Fighting Together*: This book is for anyone who is seriously courting, engaged or married. This book was written by my husband and I and we

encourage couples to fight together instead of each other.

7. *Silent Seasons*: This book is for anyone who feels like God has forgotten about them. If you're in a silent season where it seems like nothing is working out, then this book will encourage you to draw closer to the Father in the midst of this season.

Made in the USA
Lexington, KY
08 September 2018